The Yankee Journals

The Brig Nancy Ann, *of the same size and period as the* Yankee

Journals

OF TWO CRUISES ABOARD
THE AMERICAN PRIVATEER

YANKEE

---

by A Wanderer

WITH AN INTRODUCTION BY

Admiral E. M. Eller

DIRECTOR OF NAVAL HISTORY
DEPARTMENT OF THE NAVY

NEW YORK : *The Macmillan Company*
LONDON : *Collier-Macmillan Ltd.*

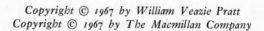

Library of Congress Catalog Card Number: 67-24289

FIRST PRINTING

The Macmillan Company, New York
Collier-Macmillan Canada Ltd., Toronto, Ontario

Printed in the United States of America

CONTENTS

ILLUSTRATIONS

INTRODUCTION

BY *Admiral E. M. Eller*
DIRECTOR OF NAVAL HISTORY
DEPARTMENT OF THE NAVY

THE War of 1812 that meant so much to America and the growth of the freedom of man fell within the giant pattern of the Napoleonic Wars. To the United States, it was the "Second War for Independence." To England, it was just a nuisance on the fringe of a life-and-death battle, a closing episode in the titanic struggle between Great Britain and France for world empire.

The principal causes of the war sprang from the impressment of American seamen, seizure of American cargo, capture of American ships, and general infringement of American rights on free international waters by the British. Hence it seems only fitting that the principal injury to England came at sea, and much of that was caused by privateers, of which the *Yankee* was among the most successful.

The major injury inflicted by the privateers was to commerce. These converted merchant ships, operated privately for a hoped-for profit, were by no means the deciding factor in the sea war, but privateers captured British merchant ships, sometimes sank them, and in general greatly hindered British use of sea highways. What life was like on board a privateer and how they operated are nowhere better illustrated than in this firsthand account of *Yankee's* first two cruises in 1812 to early 1813.

Useful though privateers were, the United States Navy itself was the deciding factor in the war. Its contributions against the powerful British Navy far outweighed the war on commerce by the privateers. Its notable victories on the high seas and Great Lakes greatly shaped America's territorial destiny; and more important, they produced unifying national pride, strengthened morale, and enduring traditions of dedication and courage.

Complex factors pushed the United States toward war. On land, the foremost was British support of the Indians of the Northwest in their effort to retain ancestral hunting grounds and check American expansion West. Yet President Madison's message of June, 1812, emphasized that British actions on the seas were the major cause of the American grievance.

Fighting desperately for life, Britain sought to weaken Napoleon by blockade. Hence their seizure and forced sale of American merchant ships and cargo, which might otherwise find their way to French hands. France had also caused large injury to American shipping in the 1790's before the United States built a small fleet and, with the *Constellation* setting the pace, in the "Quasi-War" with France (1798–1801) victoriously swept the Caribbean. After the war, France sporadically renewed depredations in an effort to halt American shipping bound for England. By official estimate, from 1803–7 France seized 389 American ships as against 528 seized by England. In succeeding years, however, England's margin of aggression widened as her navy steadily gained prominence at sea.

Indeed, as Admiral Mahan wrote, "The American found again exerted over his national commerce a control indistinguishable in practice from that of Colonial days; from what port his ships should sail, whither they might go, what cargoes they might carry, under what rules be governed in their own ports, were dictated to him as absolutely, if not in an extensive detail, as before the War of Independence."

To most Americans, far more serious than injury to trade was impressment of seamen. Locked in struggle with Napoleon, England had to have a large and superior navy. She needed seamen, and this need grew as opportunity for profit in merchant trading increased the flow of desertions from the Royal Navy. When they captured or simply searched American ships, the British found deserters from their own navy from time to time, as well as other Englishmen to impress; but they also took many Americans. When a warship's captain needed men, it was easy to stretch interpretation of the word "citizenship." As a consequence, many an American seagoing family had a member or friend dragged into servitude on a British warship. Resentment in America had sunk deep and widespread roots.

Even though the United States was divided about going to war with Britain, when war came men flocked to sea. At the time the United States Navy consisted of only a handful of ocean-going warships. Excluding condemned ships, these were: the three large 44-gun frigates of *Con-*

stitution class; three smaller 38-gun frigates, such as the *Constellation* (famous for her impressive victories in the Quasi-War with France); and ten smaller ships. As a legacy from Jefferson's misguided policy at the beginning of the century, some 62 small gunboats lay in ports along the seaboard and numerous others waited in reserve, but these had no value in open water, and little even in the restricted waters close to shore.

With these few ships, and a similar number added during the war, mostly on the Great Lake, the Americans won incredible victories. Men such as Hull, Decatur, Lawrence, Macdonough, and Perry led their ships and men to heroic feats. In an early battle, for example, the *Constitution* inspired the country by her victory over the *Guerriere*. As John Clark Ridpath wrote in his *History of the United States:* "Great . . . was the astonishment of the world when the American sailors, not waiting to be attacked, went forth without a tremor to smite the mistress of the seas."

Thrillingly for America, the *Constitution's* victory began a series of successes, with but few reverses, in single-ship combat. The victories wounded British pride and severely hampered her war effort. Sailing merchant ships had to be held up until they could be given more protection. Warships had to travel in company and blockade in force. And Britain had to expend more and more ships and men in an effort to combat the small navy of her one-time colony.

Great as the material successes were, they were overshadowed by the political and moral effects on the American people, at a time when pride, valor, and self-confidence were most needed.

The Americans had felt such emotions before, perhaps most strongly at the time of the Treaty of Paris in 1783 that proclaimed the independence of the feeble nation. But the glowing hopes of those days soon faded out. The United States had not taken an honored and respected place in international affairs. The generation brought up since Independence had witnessed a long series of oppressive, often scornful acts by nations large and small, humiliating the young, divided, and impotent country. The victories in the Quasi-War with France and the Barbary Wars soon after had stirred national spirit and somewhat strengthened ties between the loosely knit states. Yet these victories had brought short-lived rewards, and in the few years since the Barbary Wars, mounting indignities by foreign powers resulted in shame, division, and economic near-catastrophe stemming from inept political action.

To crown the humiliation, the 1812 land war against the British in weakly defended Canada started disastrously. The United States had begun this phase of the war with glowing prospects of conquest, only to have the campaign end in the defeat and surrender of its western army.

What had happened to our leaders? Couldn't the Americans fight? Had the moral stamina of 1776 faded so soon?

Here lies the real importance of the unexpected naval victories against the mighty ruler of the sea. The nation that had expected little of its infant navy against the overwhelming power of the British fleets now joined in widespread exultation over the victories. The diverse states were suddenly welded with a unifying national spirit. There was a rebirth of patriotic fervor, pride, morality. Truly, "A genuine national spirit took root and sprouted sturdily." The ship of state began to steer a true course that with inspiration from tradition of courage, dedication, integrity, hard training, and harder fighting have blessed America to this day.

In the first period of the war, England had three squadrons based on Halifax and the West Indies totaling 80 or 90 warships. These included some 11 ships of the line, 34 frigates, and numerous smaller warships. The number seems large compared with the tiny American fleet. Yet in the millions of square miles of empty sea in the western Atlantic alone, they faced giant tasks. They had to protect merchant ship convoys against both French and American attacks, guard the coast of Nova Scotia and the St. Lawrence River, patrol principal American ports against the U.S. Navy, and hunt down American warships on the high seas.

As the war progressed, and France's strength waned, England could divert a larger portion of her fleet to the American coast. So, one by one United States warships were kept in port under blockade that could not be evaded. But in the first year of the war, hard-pressed Britain could not spare the ships to effect an adequate blockade. Furthermore, having terminated the obnoxious Orders in Council that had been responsible for part of the American grievances, she did not establish blockades even against commercial ships in hopes that peace could be negotiated. After the negotiations failed, she instituted blockades in steps, by areas. The first, covering the Delaware and Chesapeake Bays and coast between, began to be effective in February, 1813. In March, the limits of the blockade were extended north to New York and south to the principal ports as far as the Mississippi River. However, needing American food-stuffs, which many U.S. citizens freely supplied, and play-ing upon New England opposition to the war, that even at times included threats of secession, Britain did not start the commercial blockade of New England ports until May, 1814.

It was thus in the early days easy enough for Americans to put to sea against the British. Supplementing the small navy, hundreds of privateers equipped themselves as best they could and joined the fight.

A privateer, as the name implies, was a privately owned vessel, operated for profit, but sailing with authority from the government. The responsibility for supplying captain and crew fell to the owner, who took his profits and paid his men hopefully from the sale of goods the privateer captured. The United States government issued letters of marque to the privateers, thus making their operation legal. They were not considered part of the navy, but supple-mented it, their value to the government coming simply from the damage they inflicted on enemy ships and the havoc they brought to enemy commerce.

Privateers, as we have noted, could not take the place of the navy. Had the United States possessed a strong navy in 1812, foreign powers would not have been so con-temptuous of her rights, and war probably would not have come. If it had been possible for the United States to enlarge her deep sea navy rapidly during the war, she would have gained far more benefit than from the privateers' efforts.

The well-trained warships of the navy went out to win control of the seas, to fight, *to serve the state*. Their dominant goal was the common good, the best advantage of the United States. Privateers sailed for profit. Some of them, like the *Yankee*, fought well indeed when they had to—as you will see from the journals. But their general aim was to avoid a real fight against anything like equal odds (again, the *Yankee* stands out for the odds it did undertake to conquer). Their dominating desire was to capture ships and cargo for personal gain. Each man who shipped out on one of them hoped his ship would be one of the few really successful cruisers, like the *Yankee*, that brought riches to crew and owners.

Interestingly, as Mahan shows in his penetrating and thorough study of the War of 1812, warships not only greatly served the state in their battles against the Royal Navy, but ship for ship they were also far more effective than privateers in commerce raiding. During the war a total of 22 ships of the U.S. Navy cruised on the ocean against the mighty British fleet. Besides their enduring service to the nation in combat, they averaged 7.5 prizes each. The 526 privateers in operation during the war averaged 2.5 prizes each.

Even though the privateers' incentive was profit, they nevertheless served the country measurably. In the two and a half years of the war they captured 1344 British ships, some heavily armed, and many only after long, heavy fighting. Most operated near the coast, from Maine to Newfoundland. Fewer went to the West Indies and fewer still ranged the high seas like the *Yankee* to face the hazards of a long voyage. Although they could not and did not take the place of an adequate navy, they did admirably support the little one we had in weakening British morale by serious injury to her commerce—the life blood of British existence, then and now.

Actually, the figure of 2.5 prizes per privateer is somewhat misleading. Of the 526 that set to sea under the American flag, three out of five returned to port empty-handed or were captured before taking any prizes. Of the 207 that captured one or more prizes in the 2½ years of war, many were captured themselves sooner or later, and only a few enjoyed outstanding success. Privateering, in other words, was a gamble and, like most gambles, often failed.

The *Yankee*, operating out of Bristol, Rhode Island, was one of the lucky few. As we read the journal of these two cruises, we can see that she deserved her luck, for with it was blended good leadership, seamanship, gunnery, discipline, courage, and skill. Only a handful of privateers captured more than a dozen prizes in the whole course of the war. During her six cruises (the first two of which are recounted in the ensuing journals—the other four were made under different captains, with different clerks), she captured a total of 40 or 41 prizes, including some 34 ships or brigs, the larger merchantmen of the time. One estimate, no doubt optimistic, places a value of $3,000,000 on the prizes and their cargoes. But even though this is probably high, excluding prizes and cargoes destroyed or recaptured, the *Yankee* must have netted several hundred thousand dollars, perhaps as much as a million. From her cruise off Africa (recounted in the second journal), as reported in Niles Register, she brought home in her own swift hull $40,000 in gold dust, 6 tons of ivory, and "32 bales of fine goods." She was a star that lured others to sea, despite the odds that brought at best no profit, or at worst capture, to many.

The *Yankee* was a brig of 168 tons, armed with a long tom, one 12-pounder, and 14 short guns (9- and 6-pounders) on her broadsides. She had a crew of 120 officers and men; for the first two voyages, her captain, so vividly described in these journals, was Oliver Wilson. According to William Armstrong Fairburn's *Merchant Sail, Vol. II,* during the war the *Yankee* was at sea for approximately eighteen months, and averaged one capture of an enemy vessel about every twelve days. An amazing record!

Thus the *Yankee* was not a typical privateer, nor are these typical journals. There are, by the very nature of the *Yankee's* exploits, more battles recounted, more adventures at farther ports recalled. Then too the journal of the second voyage is a *private* journal, not an official record (which exists, in the same handwriting, in the Rhode Island Historical Society). Here we have not only the storm, battles, and victories in the official record, but the romance of the "Wanderer" who set down his own thoughts alongside the official ones. We get people as well as events, and even poetry notable not so much for its literary merit as for its romantic flavor of the times and the insight it gives us into its author. The writer was known as Noah Jones on the ship's manifest; his real name seems to have been Noah Johnson. Literate and sensitive, his journals describe voyages that epitomize *Yankee* daring, skill, toughness in tight situations, dedication to freedom, and Christian charity in dealing with vanquished foes.

While the *Yankee* sailed off the New England coast, and later to Africa, another phase of the war was taking place on the inland waters, where the United States lacked a navy strong enough to stop the enemy short of her shores. Advancing toward Canada in the Northwest, General William Hull, uncle of the indomitable Captain Isaac Hull of the navy, produced an opposite record ashore from his famous nephew's afloat.

General Hull defeated himself by his own fears and hesitations; then General Brock, opposing the Americans, turned the defeat into disaster for them by his superb leadership, including wise and vigorous use of strength afloat. He understood that combined land and sea operations unite the unique advantages of power in ships with those especially found ashore. The result, as he demonstrated, is not simply the sum of the two, but a multiplication, often manifold. Control of the sea brings mobility, swiftness of concentration, ease of shift of objective, rapid mass transport of men and supplies, flexibility, speed, and surprise—all invaluable to any land operations.

George Washington had brought the American Revolution to victory by his vision and grand strategy in combined operations with the French Navy. As soon as France entered the war, Washington began pleading that its navy join him in attack on the main British Army. When at last the French fleet did join, the broad benefits of combined operations were of inestimable value to the United States. Admiral De Grasse's victory over the British fleet at the Chesapeake Capes, sealing Cornwallis' fate, made Yorktown and Independence possible. Still, few had realized the importance of control of the seas until General Hull learned the hard and bitter way on the Great Lakes.

In the autumn of 1812 President Madison remarked, "The command of the Lake by a superior force on the water ought to have been a fundamental part of the national policy." Although acting tardily, this country's leaders now turned in earnest to seek control of the Great Lakes. During that winter of 1812–13, naval officers directed the building of fleets on the Lakes frontiers and manned the new ships with saltwater seamen. The British also built up their Lakes squadrons, bringing in leaders from the Royal Navy. On Lake Ontario the building race resulted in a stalemate between cautious commanders. It was different on Lake Erie. There the course of America's destiny was boldly decided by Commodore Oliver Hazard Perry.

When Perry arrived on Lake Erie, March 27, 1813, construction of warships was going slowly; the shipyard lacked protection; the British commander, Barclay, was cruising Lake Erie with a superior squadron. Through remarkable force and leadership, Perry wrought a transformation and his ships sped to completion.

Having closed the gap in ships, Perry went after the enemy and in September, 1813, joined in desperate battle.

Many things went wrong—they do in war, and a measure of a great commander is how he rises to the crises. Amidst shattered ships and death Perry rose magnificently. With his flagship shot to pieces and most of his crew casualties, he embarked across the shot strewn waters, climbed on board the *Niagara*, sang out rapid orders, bore down into the enemy line firing broadsides right and left, and steered to victory: "We have met the enemy and they are ours . . ."

Control of Lake Erie made feasible successful operations ashore that would have otherwise been impossible. The United States now reaped the rich benefits control of water highways brings whether on the vast ocean or inland. More important even than the immediate military benefits were the effects on America's future. In a few hours Perry's victory had settled the question of the Northwest Territory. British threats south of Lake Erie and westward were ended for the war. The United States territorial integrity there was assured, as was the opportunity for expansion westward.

Perry's victory, of course, did not ensure United States victory in the over-all war. In fact in 1814, with Napoleon defeated, the British were unleashing a multi-pronged drive to end the war in their favor. Major operations included an attack on the Penobscot Bay area, territory the British coveted for Canada; a powerful drive down the natural highway of Lake Champlain and the Hudson River to divide dissident New England from the rest of the nation and to reopen the question of the Northwest Territory; amphibious operations to destroy supplies, shipping, and military resources throughout the inland sea of the Chesapeake Bay, and especially at Washington and Baltimore; harassing attacks in general along the whole east coast; and capture of New Orleans, with the hope of separating the vast Louisiana Territory from the United States.

Thus in the Northeast, Northwest, and Louisiana Territory, Britain sought to limit the growth and strength of the United States. Admiral Sir Alexander Cockrane, whose fleet command embraced U.S. East and Gulf Coasts, summarized British hopes. "I have it much at heart," he wrote on July 14, 1814, "to give them a complete drubbing before peace is made, when I trust their northern limits will be circumscribed and the command of the Mississippi wrested from them."

The operations against Penobscot succeeded completely. On September 1, 1814, a combined British force sailed into Castine, beginning an occupation that lasted until April 27, 1815. Had others of the main invasions been as successful, the British might have accomplished their war efforts to detach this northeastern segment of the United States.

The raiding ventures along the eastern seaboard and in the Chesapeake had likewise gone successfully for the British, culminating in the destruction of most of the small gunboats upon which Jefferson had once unwisely depended, and in the burning of Washington on August 24–25, 1814.

A different fate, however, met Admiral Cockrane's flotilla at Baltimore, when it attacked and landed troops on September 12–14, 1814, only to be repulsed in "the rocket's red glare."

The famous victory at Fort McHenry, though better known, was not as significant in a strategic sense as another victory on the Great Lakes. Only the day before Cockrane landed General Ross's troops for the assault on Baltimore, a resolute, bold, and efficient American naval officer, Commodore Thomas Macdonough, rose magnificently to his country's need in an hour of crisis on Lake Champlain. On September 6, 1814, Sir George Provost, governor-general of Canada, arrived before Plattsburg, Lake Champlain, with an army of about 11,000 men. Brigadier General Alexander Macomb had some 4,500 American regulars and militiamen to oppose him. What a handful of men can do to make combined operations remarkably effective now dramatically emerges. Macdonough had energetically built and manned a little but efficient and hard-hitting squadron. With the powerful guns of the squadron floating on the American flank, General Provost did not advance with his overwhelming army, but waited the arrival of his own naval forces.

On September 11, the British flotilla, of comparable strength to Macdonough's, came on the scene. General Provost ordered a combined attack by land and lake, but held back ashore awaiting decision afloat. In a brilliant hard-fought action, Macdonough drove to victory routing the British ships. He humbly reported, "The Almighty has been pleased to grant us a signal victory."

Seeing no hope of success without control of the "Inland Sea," Provost promptly retired to Canada. Macdonough's stirring victory had ended the gravest threat of the war. Provost's army of veterans of the Napoleonic Wars with

their overwhelming numbers might otherwise have cut the
United States in two along the Hudson to New York. Had
this happened the United States might have been forced
to unhappy, perhaps disastrous, territorial concessions in
the peace negotiations then underway. Fewer than 1,000
Americans in a handful of ships had changed the course of
history.

The victory not only prevented invasion of the American north, it made continuation of the war by the British
in the area impossible, except at prodigious effort. This
stands out clearly in the words of England's greatest military commander of the century and conqueror of Napoleon, the Duke of Wellington. When news of the British
defeat on Lake Champlain reached England, Wellington
was offered the command in America. His reply shows
something of his common sense and wisdom. Neither he
nor anyone else, he said, could conquer from Canada without control of the Lakes. The British needed, he added,
"not a general, nor general officers and troops," but
superiority afloat on the lakes:

> Till that superiority is acquired, it is impossible, ac-
> cording to my notion, to maintain an army in such
> a situation as to keep the enemy out of the whole
> frontier, much less to make any conquest from the
> enemy, which, with those superior means, might,
> with reasonable hopes of success, be undertaken.
> . . . The question is, whether we can obtain this
> naval superiority on the lakes. If we cannot, I shall
> do you but little good in America; and I shall go
> there only to prove the truth of Provost's defense,

and to sign a peace which might as well be signed now.

Elsewhere ashore the benefits of the sea entered into the few important victories. In the glorious defence of Fort McHenry on September 13, contingents of sailors had played a gallant role. Manning batteries with seaman-like skill and sturdiness, they punished the British severely. Meanwhile at Norfolk, the *Constellation* drained off of some of the British ships which could have added important guns against Fort McHenry.

A most notable direct contribution to operations ashore was by Commodore Patterson in General Jackson's victory at New Orleans after the peace treaty had been signed. In this truly combined operation the influence of a small group of sailors far outweighed their numbers. Commodore Daniel T. Patterson's little squadron fought so valiantly and effectively that they surely made the difference between potential American disaster and actual American victory.

England fought the tyranny of France; America fought the tyranny of England; and in the strange working of their diverse plans, both furthered freedom. In defeating Napoleon, England brought about her own golden age of the nineteenth century. Bright jewel in this golden age was the spread of freedom, and one of the major avenues of freedom is the seas. Britain wanted the seas free of French harassment; in standing up for the principle, she fought for precisely what the United States was also fighting—against her.

In standing up for the freedom of the sea and rights of

men against impressment—a practice little short of slavery
—the United States was preparing for its eventual leadership on the seas. The lessons it learned from the War of
1812 were fixed in the national consciousness. Humiliating
blockade, economic strangulation, amphibious attacks, pil-
lage, and destruction, including the burning of the capital
of government, were bitter lessons indeed, but they taught
Americans that oceans are barriers to enemies only if *one
is strong on them.*

We learned the lesson in 1812–15; we might have
learned it in the battle of the Chesapeake Capes that led to
the victory at Yorktown. For as Washington said then, "It
follows then as certain as that night succeeds the day, that
without a decisive naval force we can do nothing definitive.
And with it—everything honourable and glorious."

Even while reading and thrilling over the *Yankee's*
exploits against large odds of capture by the British Navy,
we should remember Washington's words that were as pro-
phetic of the centuries ahead as they were accurate at the
time. Every important struggle in which the United States
has engaged since then has likewise depended on this ancient
power from the ocean. This points a truth of utmost sig-
nificance for the United States as she leads the world into
a future that cannot be great unless she holds the sea.

EDITOR'S NOTE

Who was the "Wanderer" who recorded the first two of six cruises of the *Yankee* during the War of 1812? On the *Yankee* manifest he is listed as Noah Jones, ship's clerk, yet in all probability his real name was Noah Johnson, an ancestor of Mrs. Johnson Pratt whose son, William V. Pratt, owns the journals and submitted them for publication. For on the title page of the original journals, the name "Noah Johnson" is written in a faint but legible hand, and it is improbable that the journals would have become part of the records of the Johnson family were the author not a Johnson himself.

Why, then, the change of name? It is impossible to be sure, but the likelihood is, to judge from the internal evidence of the second journal, that Noah Johnson was something of a black sheep—and entirely a romantic. Pseudonyms were common among those who went to sea (especially if they undertook the hazardous and not-too-many-questions-asked life aboard a privateer), and Noah Johnson, had a knack for self-dramatization, a knack that becomes quickly clear as you read the second journal with its references to "Horatio" (himself), its melodramatic poetry, its theatrical style.

The second journal is, in fact, quite different in tone and content from the first. Obviously Johnson wrote the first as a ship's log, a formal record of what turned out to be a highly successful adventure. It has a signed letter from the *Yankee* commander, Captain Oliver Wilson, attesting to its truthfulness; its fascination is historical, not personal. Equally obvious, however, is that he meant the second to be his own *private* record, a record of feeling as well as event.

A formal record of the second cruise, also kept by Johnson (or Jones) exists. The original is in the Rhode Island Historical Society in Providence, but it was largely excerpted by Professor Wilfred H. Munro in two books, *The Most Successful American Privateer* (American Antiquarian Society, The Davis Press, 1913) and *Tales of an Old Sea Port* (Princeton University Press, 1917), both out of print but available in some libraries if you want to make a comparison of the texts.

When Mr. Pratt sent in photographic copies of the journals (he kept the originals in a safe deposit box in a Bangor, Maine, bank), neither he nor I was aware that a formal record existed: we both assumed that the second journal was simply a fanciful ship's log written as it was to enliven what is often a tedious record-keeping chore. I discovered Professor Munro's books during a research trip to Bristol, Rhode Island, where the *Yankee* was built and from where it sailed. The language in the journal reprinted by Munro and that in the copy in my possession were in places so similar as to leave little doubt that the two journals had been written by the same man (or that one

Bristol R.I. July 11th 1812

Sir,

Agreeably to the Act of Congress concerning Letters of marque, and reprisals Prizes and Prize Goods. we have to request you as the person employed by the Secretary of State a commission for the Brig called the Yankee. burthen one hundred and sixty tons. mounting Eighteen guns, owned by James DWolf and John Smith both of Bristol in the county of Bristol and State of Rhode Island — the Crew to consist of One hundred and ten persons to cruize on the high seas

J. W. DWolf

John Smith

To Charles Collins Esqr—
Collector for the Port of Bristol

Letter from J. W. D'Wolf and John Smith,
owners of the Yankee, requesting a
commission for the brig

had been copied from the other), yet in the printed journal there was none of the romance or mysticism in the journal I had, and none of the liveliness of style.

We had, of course, sent the first and second journals to a handwriting expert immediately upon receiving them. He had verified them as being of the period of 1812. But now questions arose. Why would a man keep *two* journals that were so similar? Had the version we possessed been copied and embellished by someone other than the author for some unknown reason? Did we, in fact, own a fake?

A call to the American Antiquarian Society in Worcester, Massachusetts, did little to relieve the anxiety. It was almost inconceivable, we were told, that a ship's clerk would keep two journals, for what would be the purpose of it. And there was no doubt that the journal printed by Professor Munro was authentic. What we most likely had was a clever forgery, so good as to deceive a handwriting expert, but probably written some years after the actual cruises and patently not written by the ship's clerk himself.

Despite their skepticism, the Society agreed to let us bring the manuscript to them so they could at least double-check the date of the documents. Accordingly, a representative from Mr. Pratt's bank took down the originals of the journals—and again, the verdict was positive: the journals *were* written by the same man. If the first was a true ship's log (as so sworn to by Captain Wilson), then the second was also written by the clerk.

As a final check, we had the journals shipped to the Rhode Island Historical Society in Providence for a comparison of the handwriting with the handwriting of the original journals excerpted by Professor Munro. The hand-writing was the same. For some unknown reason, Noah Johnson/Jones wrote *two* versions of the second cruise of the *Yankee*, whereas he had kept only one version—the one reprinted here—of the first. Whatever his motives—and it is possible he visualized publication of the "private" journal, but probably not 155 years later—the journal is authentic, with all its vividness, splendor, excitement, enthusiasm, joy, and despair.

The "private" second journal covers 106 of the 150 days of the voyage—the return to America is omitted, although covered in the public record. Fittingly, it ends with the capture of yet one more prize, the *Harriot & Matilda*. The *Yankee* was the most successful of all American privateers. On May 20, 1813, she embarked on a third cruise, under Captain Elisha Snow, returning to port on August 20. The fourth cruise began in September, 1813, under Captain Thomas Jones; the fifth in May 1814 (the delay was caused by a strict blockade imposed by the British off Rhode Island) again under Captain Snow; and the sixth in October, 1814, under Captain William C. Jenks. In all, the *Yankee* was at sea for slightly over 18 months, and averaged the capture of an enemy vessel about every twelve days!

There is no indication that Noah Johnson sailed on any beyond the first two cruises. What his fate was after the second cruise ended no one knows. Our only record of him is these two journals.

But at least we have these documents, valuable first because of the picture they give of life aboard a privateer

during the painful war with Great Britain—and second
because of the picture they give of "a wanderer," whose
heart will still "beat responsive to the ties of kindred affection and vibrate to all the softer passions of the soul."

In most cases we have remained true to the original
spelling and punctuation of the journals, changing only
when we felt an antique spelling would be unknown to
modern readers or when a change in punctuation would
appreciably clarify a sentence or notation. Even the small
fists indicating new paragraphs appearing in the first part
of this book are reproductions of those in the handwritten
journal.

Acknowledgment is due first to Mr. William V. Pratt,
president of the Arctic Belle Mining Company, who
brought these journals to our attention; then to Mr. F. M.
O'Brien of the American Antiquarian Bookseller's Associa-
tion, to Clifford K. Shipton, director of the American
Antiquarian Society, and to Clarkson A. Collins 3rd, librar-
ian of the Rhode Island Historical Society, for their invaluable help in authenticating the journals; to Karl and Samuel
Philbrick, George L. Howe, Elena Shute, Roland Howard,
and Norman S. Feister for their contributions to the at-
tendant research on the journals; and most particularly to
Admiral E. M. Eller for his support and cooperation well
beyond the preparation of his excellent introduction.

Journal

OF THE FIRST CRUISE

❊

Commencing July 15th, 1812

Journal
Of a Cruise on board the
Private Armed Vessel of War,
Called

The Yankee.

Oliver Wilson
Commander.

Commencing July 15th 1812

The title page of the first journal

The First Cruise

¶

At 8 A.M. got under weigh and beat out of the harbour, the wind S.W. and the tide at flood. As we passed Fort Wolcott fired a salute of three guns, which was answered by raising the American standard. At 9 A.M. passed Rhode Island Light from which we took our departure for Holmes' Hole. Course E.S.E.—fresh gales, cloudy weather, squalls and rain. At ½ past 11 A.M. Gay-head Light bore S. by E. ½ S. At meridian observed a schooner ahead, distant about a league; as she showed no colours and crowded all sail to avoid speaking us, fired a six pound shot under her stern and immediately set the fore-royal, fore and fore-top gallant studding sails and main gaff topsail in chase. Upon which the schooner hoisted American coulors and bore away for Quick's Hole. At 2 P.M. anchored in Holmes' Hole.

¶

2ᵈ day   *Thursday 16ᵗʰ, July 1812*

Weighed anchor at ½ past 5 A.M. bound for Falmouth, distant 3 leagues. The wind N.W. with fresh gales and cool weather. At 7 A.M. came to in Falmouth harbour. The commander and his clerk went on shore and opened a rendezvous for volunteers. Enlisted 4 fine fellows—came on board and fired a salute of 2 guns. At 5 P.M. again weighed anchor on our return to Holmes' Hole. Wind westerly, moderate and pleasant. All drawing sails set, except the stay-sails.

☞ It is worthy of particular observation that the brig ran from Falmouth harbour to Holmes' Hole, a distance of 9 miles, in 31 minutes, although the tide was part of the time against us. At 6 P.M. exercised all hands at the musket, and at sundown regulated the several messes on board. At 8 P.M. hailed the sloop *Resolution*, which came to anchor a short distance on our weather quarter from Boston, and sent our boat with the first lieutenant on board, who reported on his return that upwards of 40 privateers had already sailed from the eastern ports, that 7 prizes had been sent into Boston, that a French ship had arrived from France with brandy, that a British brig of war was cruising off the port and had sent several prizes into Halifax, besides robbing many others of money and other effects.

N.B.: Samuel Slocum, one of the gunner's mates, on being commanded by Captain Wilson to perform his duty in the capacity for which he shipped, replied, "I will not," and made use of various other mutinous expressions. For which disorderly and mutinous conduct the Commander thought it adviseable to reprimand him severely and sent him on shore.

¶

3ᵈ day   *Friday 17ᵗʰ, July 1812*

From 8 to 10 A.M. exercised the men at the great guns and small arms, and went through the various maneuvers of boarding an enemy's vessel over the bows, midships and stern. At meridian the first lieutenant and clerk went on board the brig *Harriet* of Boston. They were informed that she was 29 days out from Cayenne bound home, that she had traded at several ports on the coast of Brazil, that there were no British men of war on the station, that upwards of 200 sail of English merchantmen [were] either trading at or bound home from said coast, that they were badly armed and had very few men, and most of those either boys or invalids. At 1 P.M. got under weigh, with two pilots on board, bound over Nantucket shoals. Light breezes, with pleasant weather and a smooth sea. At 4 P.M. Nantucket Light bore due S. distant 2 leagues. At 5 P.M. discharged the pilots—all drawing sails set. Course E.S.E., wind W.S.W., run 8½ knots per log. At same time Tom's-Never-head bluff bore S.S.W., distant 4 leagues. From which land we took our departure bound out to sea upon a cruise, with 78 prime fellows on board and the ship in complete order. Secured the boat, the anchors and great guns, cleared the deck and quartered the men in three watches. Several sails in sight supposed to be coasters bound into Boston.

¶

4ᵗʰ day   *Saturday 18ᵗʰ, July 1812*

At sunrise David Price, a seaman, called out from the fore-top, a sail to windward, S. by W. ¼ W. distant about 5 leagues. Immediately made all sail in chase, upon which the strange sail altered her course from E. by S. and hauled close upon a wind. At 7 P.M. tacked ship to the westward. At 8 P.M. again tacked ship to the S.E. Called all hands to quarters, loaded the cannon on both sides, drew up the marines in line of battle, armed the officers and company with swords, pistols, muskets, cutlasses, blunderbusses, boarding pikes, battle axes, etc., and prepared to give the enemy two broadsides and then to board her. At 10 P.M. came along side and sent the first lieutenant on board, who returned with the ships papers, from which it appeared that she was an American ship called *The White Oak*, Ezekiel Onslow, master, from Portsmouth, New Hampshire, 2 days out bound to Puerto Rico, with a full cargo of lumber, brandy and provisions. Her clearance, license and other documents were regularly executed. Suspecting said ship to have a British license, the commander sent the first and third lieutenants, clerk and first mate with several hands on board to examine said vessel, with orders to take charge of her and send her into port. After a strict examination, not being able to discover any cause of capture, permitted her to proceed on her voyage.

At 11 P.M. again made sail. Course E., wind southerly, light breezes, pleasant weather and smooth sea. 6 knots per log.

Latitude Observation 41° 5′

¶

5th day *Sunday 19th, July 1812*

During these 24 hours light winds and calm with flying clouds. At 5 P.M. Henry Mikele discovered a sail ahead, distant about 4 leagues; set all sail in chase. At ½ past 5 P.M., James Brown saw a sail to the leeward. At 6 P.M. the same man saw another sail abeam, distant 5 leagues. At 8 P.M. the first lieutenant and clerk boarded the ship *Jane* of New York, James Selkerk, master, in ballast, 43 days out from Cadiz bound home. Were informed that she was spoke in Cadiz bay by a squadron of English merchantmen bound to the provinces, that on the 7th instant, Latitude 43° she was boarded by an officer from a British letter-of-marque ship from St. Thomas' bound to Liverpool, that on the 10th first she spoke an English brig with lumber from Halifax bound home. At ½ past 8 P.M., tacked ship to the S.S.W. At 10 P.M., 5 sail in sight. At meridian boarded the schooner *William Thatcher* of Dartmouth, from Cadiz bound to New Bedford. Said schooner spoke an English merchantman off the Azores bound to the eastward. Also boarded the schooner *Richmond*, Cranston Nevins, master, from Oporto, 41 days out bound to Rhode Island. The *Richmond* spoke no vessels and brings no news; left a great many American vessels and 4 English men of war at Cadiz.

Latitude Observation 41° 9′ — Longitude D.R. 66° 6′

¶

6ᵗʰ day *Monday 20ᵗʰ, July 1812*

At 1 A.M. made sail. Course E. by N., wind southerly, cloudy and squally, with thunder and rain. Took in all sail except the fore topsail and scud before the wind. At 4 o'clock the weather moderated and we made sail again. At 5 tacked ship. Course E. by N. At ½ past 6 saw a sail ahead. At 7 A.M. the first lieutenant and clerk boarded her. She proved to be the schooner *Traveller*, Henry Richards, master, 31 days from Cadiz, bound to New York with ballast and a few casks of drugs. As the vessel had no name on her stern and the bill of lading did not mention the particular articles on board, we directed the boxes to be opened by permission of the captain and in presence of several of his people: found they contained only Peruvian bark, camphor, etc., but no contraband or English goods. The captain informed us he had spoken only one vessel, a fisherman near the Great Bank, who said that all the fishermen had been ordered home by a frigate which arrived there a few days before. Captain Richards had not heard of the Declaration of War, neither had the vessels we boarded yesterday. At ½ past 9 P.M. James Askey called out a sail two points upon the beam, steering to the westward. Supposing her to be another Cadiz prize kept on our course with all drawing sails set.

Latter part fair and pleasant; 7 knots per log.

Latitude Observation 41° 20′ — Longitude 64° 0′

¶

7th day *Tuesday 21st, July 1812*

Commences with moderate breezes and pleasant weather. At ½ past 9 P.M. saw a sail to the windward. Called all hands to quarters and stationed the men at their guns. Fired three shots, tacked ship twice and at 12 midnight came along side and sent our boat on board. Found her to be the English schooner *Mary Ann* from Halifax, a prize to the *Buckskin*, American privateer. She came out of Cape Sable on Saturday and was captured on Sunday. She was loaded with tar and has nine female passengers on board. Our men, both seamen and marines, stood near two hours at their quarters and performed their respective evolutions with great order and regularly. Lieutenant Sweet was informed that no armed vessels of war had yet sailed from Halifax and that there were few vessels in port, but a great number [were] expected from England and the British islands. The *Buckskin* is fitted out from Salem, mounts only one gun, had 40 men on board when she sailed, has taken 5 prizes but of no great value.

Latter part light breezes and calm with smooth sea. All hands employed about their customary duty.

Latitude Observation 42° 6′

¶

8ᵗʰ day   *Wednesday 22ᵈ, July 1812*

First part pleasant weather with light winds. At 3 A.M. saw a sail ahead. Set all sails in chase. At 5, observing that the sail was using her sweeps, got out the brig's on the starboard side and found they assisted her greatly. At ½ past 7 came up with said sail and fired a gun to the leeward, which she answered in the same manner and hoisted American colours. Our commander then ordered her to ware ship and come under our lee. Found her to be the American privateer pilotboat-built schooner *Regulator* of Salem, commanded by James Mansfield, mounting 2 guns with 30 or 40 men, 15 days out upon a cruise; had retaken one American vessel and sent another in on suspicion, loaded with hardware. Captain Mansfield informed us that the *Regulator* had been chased by three British cruisers at different times, and that one of them recaptured a prize while in his possesion. Captain Mansfield further mentioned that the *Dolphin*, privateer fitted out from Salem, had taken seven prizes and among others a British West India letter-of-marque ship, mounting 16 guns, loaded with 400 hogsheads of sugar. The *Dolphin* took her by the following stratagem. The captain of the privateer went on board the ship, declared his vessel to be a British tender, invited the English captain on board the privateer, immediately ran along side and boarded her without losing a man.

At 9 P.M. discovered a sail upon our weather beam. At ½ past 10 fired one of the bow guns and the vessel immediately hove to. At 11 sent the boat on board; found her to be the American brig *Montesuma*, Captain Crawford, from Waterford, Ireland, bound to Bath, 42 days out in ballast. The *Montesuma* spoke the American squadron, Commodore Rogers on the 5th July in Latitude 45° N. and Longitude 33° W. They informed Captain Crawford of the war and said the squadron had taken and *burnt* 21 English vessels, one of them being a fine corvette brig. The squadron had seen no vessels of war. Captain Crawford spoke no English vessels and brings no news.

Latitude Observation 42° 3′ — Longitude D.R. 60° 40′

¶

9 days out   *Thursday 23ᵈ, July 1812*

The day begins with light breezes and cloudy weather. Course E.S.E. bound for Corvo, the northwesternmost of the Azores; our commander thinking it adviseable to proceed to the coast of Brazil, our cruising station, by looking in at the western islands and obtaining supplies if necessary, passing by Madeira and the Canaries, and running down between the coast of Africa and the Cape De Vert Islands. Middle part calm. At ½ past 10 P.M. John Chace called out from aloft a sail 1½ points on our lee bow, distant about 5 leagues. At ½ past 11 fired the larbord bow gun and piped all hands to quarters; upon which the sail wore ship and run down under our lee. Sent our boat on board and found her to be the ship *Tiphys* of Bath, Ezekiel Puranton, master, 37 days out from Liverpool bound to Boston, in ballast. On the 5th July the *Tiphys* spoke an English ship from Jamaica bound to London. On the 19th saw Sable Island. Judges himself to day in Long. 62° 50′. Captain Puranton informed us that there were 12 sail of English merchantmen loading in Liverpool bound out to Newfoundland by Halifax, that one of them sailed the day before the *Tiphys* [and] the remainder were to sail in a few days. That they were loaded with full cargoes, were all of them armed, but had few men and those mostly boys and foreigners. No news. Latter part very pleasant with gentle breezes and a clear sky.

Latitude Observation 42° 2′ — Longitude D.R. 60° 4′

¶

10 days out   *Friday 24ᵗʰ, July 1812*

Pleasant gales and fine weather. Course E. by N. 4 knots. Wind southerly. At ½ past 4 A.M. Richard Raven discovered a sail from aloft bearing S.E. by E. ½ E., distant 4 leagues. At 6 supposed the sail to be an English ship of war, as she hauled up close upon the wind in chase of us, set all her canvass, and showed her colours, which we mistook for signals. At 7 observing that the sail gave over the chase and kept away, we immediately tacked ship resolved to know what she was, at 8 sent our boat on board and found her to be the brig *Elisa & Mary* of Salem from Cadiz 33 days out, bound home. The captain informed us that on the 14th instant in Longitude 45° 59′, he was boarded by a British frigate, and that about 7 days ago he spoke an English brig to the westward of St. Michaels with a full Cargo of wine, bound to the St. Lawrence. At 12 midnight saw a sail under our lee, piped all hands to quarters, fired two guns and gave chase. At 1 P.M. boarded the brig *William & Martha* of Boston, 49 days out from Liverpool bound, to Amelia Island with a cargo of salt. Ordered the captain with his papers on board the privateer—about 20 days ago the *William & Martha* was boarded by an English armed vessel of war; yesterday she saw several sail standing to the westward. There were upwards of 50 American vessels lying at Liverpool and a number of English merchant ships loading for the West Indies and the Brazils and nearly ready for sea. At 7 P.M. John Chace saw a sail ahead bearing E.S. Set sail in chase. At 10 observing that the sail ahead was an armed sloop, with American colours, distant about 1 mile, and believing her to be one of the American privateers, gave up the chase and hauled up on our course. The latter part of these 24 brisk gales, cloudy and cold weather.

Latitude Observation 43° 13′ — Longitude D.R. 58°

¶

11 days out   Saturday *25ᵗʰ, July 1812*

These 24 hours commence with stiff gales and cloudy weather. Wind S.W. to S. Course E. to N. At 2 A.M. double reefed the square foresail, lowered down the fore and aft fore sail and took off the bonnet, sent down the top gallant yard, housed the top gallant mast, sent down the main-top-mast, secured the boats, lashed the great guns, and got everything ready for a blow. At 9 lowered down the mainsail and hove to under the three-reefed foresail and topsail. Shipped a great deal of water upon deck. At 6 sound in 28 fathoms water off the Isle of Sables. Sent up top gallant mast; let the reefs out of the mainsail, foresail and fore-top sail. Latter part light winds, with heavy swell and dark foggy weather.

No Observation

¶

12 days out *Sunday 26th, July 1812*

First and middle part, light winds and a thick fog with a heavy swell. Latter part a clear horizon and pleasant weather. No sail in sight. Course E.N.E. Wind southerly averaged 4 knots.

The captain and lieutenant of marines have been on the sick list most part of the time since we left port.

Latitude Observation 44° 33' — Longitude D.R. 57° 7'

¶

13 days out *Monday 27th, July 1812*

At 8 P.M. James Askey called out from the mast head a sail bearing 1½ points on our lee bow. At ½ past 8 Master Snow saw a sail from the quarter deck bearing N.E. to N.

It being nearly calm, got out our sweeps in chase of the brig, and found we could row her at the rate of four knots per hour. At 12 meridian run under the lee of the brig, and ordered her to lower her colours, she having hoisted the English flag, which she did accordingly. Sent our boat on board and found her to be the British brig *Alfred of Tinmouth*; Captain James Trueman, from Havre Grace, Newfoundland, in ballast, bound to Brunswick, navigated by a captain, mate, 4 seamen and a boy. Finding the said brig to be old, out of repair, poorly rigged, and not worth sending into port, our commander ordered us to take out of her, all the water, provisions, furniture, cabin stores and other valuable articles, and then set her on fire; which we performed accordingly. At 2 A.M. on Tuesday we sent the prisoners on board our brig and set the *Alfred* on fire as above mentioned. We then tacked in chase of the ship.

No Observation

☞ The above brig was armed with 24 pounders with powder shot.

¶

14 days out   *Tuesday 28th, July 1812*

At ½ past 3 A.M. we saw our prize sink after having burnt upwards of an hour and a half. She was built at Exeter, measured 152½ tons, was 14 years old, formerly carried

8 guns and 16 men, and was employed in the coal trade. She brought out a cargo of salt to Havre Grace and was bound to Brunswick for a cargo of lumber. Her hull was still sound and her standing rigging pretty good, but her sails and running rigging were miserable. We took out of her 2 iron four pounders, one of which we intend to mount in the bows of the Barge, and also a very fine jolly-boat, which we retained instead of our own, setting ours adrift. Upon the whole we were all of the opinion that the *Alfred* would not have paid the expense of condemnation, if sent into port.

Our commander, in obedience to those humane instructions he received from government, permitted the prisoners to remain at large, invited Captain Trumain to mess in the cabin, directed the officers of the wardroom to receive the mate in their mess, ordered a separate mess of the other prisoners and gave them a full allowance of provisions.

After having tacked in chase of the ship in the morning, it died away nearly a calm and the usual fog completely encompassed the vessel, so that we gave over the chase and tacked again on our usual course of E.N.E. Winds westerly; thick fog with rain. The brig has averaged about 2 knots per hour. Lieutenant Sweet having selected proper persons to man the barge & jolly-boat when sent to search an enemy's vessel, and appointed Moses Cromwell Coxswain of the barge and Lewis Cooper of the jolly-boat, the commander issued particular instructions regulating their conduct upon such occasions, the manner in which any property taken should be divided and prohibiting under severe penalties all dishonest behavior.

Latitude Observation 46° 6′ — Longitude D.R. 55°
soundings 25 fathoms

¶

15 days out   *Wednesday 29th, July 1812*

At 5 P.M. Isaac Butler saw a sail bearing W.N.W. distant
about 2 miles, and Master Snow discovered another sail
bearing N.E. by N. distant about 3 miles. Immediately
piped all hands to quarters, got out our sweeps, set all sail
and luffed up in pursuit of the windward sail. It being
foggy with light winds, [we] soon lost sight of both sails.
At 8 we again saw the first mentioned sail bearing S.W.
distant 8 miles, standing to the N.W. At 10 called all hands
to quarters again, got ready for action and run down under
the lee of a large armed English brig, ordered her to lower
her colours instantly or we should fire into her, which she
did accordingly. Sent the boat on board with Lieutenant
Sweet with orders to take possession of her, send the prisoners on board and follow us. Found her to be the English
copper-bottomed brig *Harmony*, Captain William Gammil,
217 58/94 tons burthen, mounting 4 carriage guns and
navigated by 18 men, from Greenock bound to Quebec,
with a cargo of rum, linens, manufactured iron, tobacco,
ale, merchandise and sundries. The *Harmony* and cargo
may be reasonably estimated at $40,000. The commander
sent Captain Rufus Burr with a quarter-master and seven

seamen on board the *Harmony*, gave him a regular commission, letter of instructions, the brig's papers and letters to the owners and ordered him to make the best of his way into Bristol. At 11 tacked ship in chase of another brig to the windward, fired several guns, upon which she bore away for us. Sent Lieutenant Russell on board with orders to send the prisoners and brig's papers on board the privateer and follow her. Found the last mentioned prize to be the English copper-fastened brig *Henry*, Captain Mathew Glover, 180 tons burthen, mounting 2 guns with 8 men, from Sunderland in ballast bound to the St. Lawrence. The *Henry* is a fine new brig, only 12 months old, completely rigged and in good order, and may be worth $6,000. Our commander sent George Eddy on board as prize master with a mate and 5 seamen, and ordered her into Bristol with the same instructions as the *Harmony*. At ½ past 11 Richard Raven saw a sail ahead, set all sail in chase and shortly after captured her as will appear in the next day's journal.

At meridian saw land from the mast head, supposed it to be Cape St. Mary's.

Latitude Observation 46° 18′ — Longitude 55° 33′

¶

16 days out   *Thursday 30ᵗʰ, July 1812*

At 2 A.M. we captured the brig *Mary*, 208 tons burthen, bound to Newfoundland in ballast. The *Mary* not being a valuable vessel and having 4 captains and 43 prisoners on board the *Yankee*, and not wishing to keep them on board, or send them to America, the commander thought proper to make them a present of the *Mary*, on condition of their subscribing an oath not to serve against the United States in any capacity whatsoever, during the present war, but to consider themselves as prisoners of war and liable to be exchanged man for man when an exchange of prisoners should take place, and further that they should immediately proceed up St. George's Channel to the Firth of Clyde and not touch at any port in North America. Kept company with our prizes during the night. Light winds and pleasant weather. At 10 P.M. fresh breezes from the S.S.E. Course S.W. by W. Soon lost sight of the *Henry* and *Harmony* astern.

Latitude Observation 45° 22′

¶

17 days out *Friday 31ˢᵗ, July 1812*

These 24 hours light winds, clear sky, smooth sea and pleasant weather. At 1 A.M. tacked ship to the eastward. At 2 saw our prize the *Harmony*, distant 4 leagues to the leeward; the *Henry* was also visible from aloft. At 10 Isaac Butler called out from masthead a sail bearing E. by N. ½ N. distant about 5 leagues. Set all sail in chase. At 11 saw land, supposed to be Cape Pine. At ½ past 10 George

Disley saw another sail bearing N.E. Got out all the sweeps in chase of the first mentioned vessel and rowed the brig at the rate of 3 knots per hour. At meridian we were still in chase of a large English ship, distant about 4 miles upon the lee bow. The land all in sight from deck.

¶

18 days out   *Saturday 1st, August 1812*

At 1 A.M. we prepared for action and ran down upon the weather quarter of the ship mentioned in yesterday's journal, who filled away and also prepared for action. We immediately fired our 1st Division, upon which the ship returned a broadside, and the action became general. The officers and marines poured into the enemy a full volley of musquetry, and the three divisions. At the same time gave her a broadside. We then bore away, run athwart his bows, gave him another broadside, which raked him fore and aft and discharged all the small arms. During this time, however, the enemy kept up a well directed fire, shot away some of our rigging and wounded two of our men. But we soon completely destroyed her standing and running rigging and sails, killed the helsman and kept up so warm a fire of round, langrage, cannister, grape, musket balls, buckshot and pistol bullets, that the enemy's ship became unmanageable and she came down bows upon us. We instantly sheered off, gave her another full discharge of all our arms, and prepared to board her with boarding pikes, muskets, cutlasses and pistols, when the enemy hawled down his colours. The firing then ceased and we gave the enemy three cheers. Sent Lieutenant Sweet with an armed boat's crew on board and took possession of her. She proved to be the English ship *Royal Bounty*, Captain Henry Gambles, 353 tons burthen, mounting 10 carriage guns, with powder, shot, muskets, cutlasses and pistols. She was from Hull 7 weeks out bound to Prince Edward's Island. On boarding her we found one man killed, the captain, two mates, boatswain, cook and one seaman dangerously wounded. That we had shot away nearly all her standing and running rigging, stove her boats, damaged her sails, masts and spars and pierced her hull and bulworks with a great many shot both large and small. Her mainsail received 153 shot of different kinds, her maintopsail and indeed all her other sails were so completely cut to pieces as to be unserviceable. Even her colours were penetrated with six musket shot.

We regret to mention that two of our own seamen, namely, Aaron Mason Boatswain's, first mate, and John Chace, quartermaster, were badly wounded though not dangerously. The prisoners were taken on board the privateer and the wounded dressed by our surgeon.

At 4 P.M. saw a brig in shore of us, gave chase and at ½ past 5 came alongside of her. Found she was deserted by her officers and crew, who had plundered her of all valuable articles, taken to their long-boat and made for the land, during our engagement with the *Royal Bounty*. Discovered by her log, which we found on board, that she was the brig *Thetis*, 136 tons burthen, loaded with coal; thinking her of little value, the commander with the consent of his officers, ordered her to be set on fire, which was done accordingly. We then stood for the *Royal Bounty*, and after taking out of her sundry small articles of no great value, she was also set on fire. The *Royal Bounty* being a Dutch clump built vessel, and in so shattered a condition as to be unmanageable, the commander and officers did not think her worth sending into port.

The prisoners, 24 in number, then on board the *Yankee*, solicited the commander to give them the Ship's [sideboat] and permit them to go on shore, being within two leagues of St. Mary's Bay, which he did immediately, supplying them with all kinds of necessaries for their departure. At 11 o'clock, being a fine night with a smooth sea, the [sideboat] left us, proceeded for the land and we made sail to the southward.

We lament to state that Carlos Bucetti, one of our seamen, being on board the *Royal Bounty* at the time she was set on fire, became intoxicated and fell into the ship's hold; great exertions were made to relieve him but without effect, as he was probably killed by the fall.

The commander was highly gratified in observing the greatest emulation and activity both in the officers and company as well upon this as all other occasions. Their readiness to attend quarters, to obey orders, exercise their guns, and go through the ship's duty merit his applause. He feels the greatest reliance upon their courage and fortitude in the day of battle, "which tries men's souls," and had no doubt but their endeavors will always be crowned with Fortune and Victory.

¶

19 days out   *Sunday 2ᵈ, August 1812*

These 24 hours commence with stiff gales and rainy weather. At 1 A.M. took in all the sight sails, and square foresail, reefed the foretopsail and mainsail, sent down main-top gallant mast, fore royal and topgallant yard, housed the royal and topgallant mast, secured the boats and guns, and prepared for bad weather. At 11 A.M. tacked ship to the southward. Heavy rain, cold and extremely dark. Sounded but got no bottom. At 2 tacked ship to the east-ward. At 8 P.M. the weather moderated, sent up the main-topmast, royal and topgallant yards, let out all the reefs, and set the square-foresail, fore topgallant sail and fore-staysail. At 11 saw a large island of ice, under the lee dis-tant about 4 miles. Latter part moderate breezes and foggy weather. The commander divided the spoil taken on board the *Royal Bounty* among the crew. No sail in sight. In-valids in a fair way to recover and the crew generally in good health and spirits.

Latitude Observation 46° 13′

¶

20 days out   *Monday 3ᵈ, August 1812*

First part moderate breezes with foggy and rainy weather. All hands employed in splicing and mending the rigging and repairing the damage received in the action with the *Royal Bounty*. At 6 thick and foggy with heavy rain. At ½ past 6 Sylvanus Goff called out from the bows, "Ice ahead." Immediately called all hands upon deck and soon discovered it to be land, distant about a mile. Wore ship instantly and stood off to the southward. The land we saw was Cape Race, barren, rocky and mountainous. At 8 sounded in 35 fathoms water. At 10 in 42 fathoms. At 11 in 46 fathoms. At midnight in 57 fathoms. At 1 P.M. in 50 fathoms. At 2 close reefed the foretopsail and single reefed the mainsail sent down topgallant yard and maintopmast and took in fore aft foresail. At 8 P.M. let out the reefs and set fore aft foresail. Middle part excessively dark with heavy rain. Latter part more moderate with a thick wet fog. Course E. by S. Average 4 knots. At meridian sound winded in 70 fathoms. Mason, Chace and Walker, the invalids, improving in health.

No Observation — Longitude D.R. 53° 37′

¶

21 days out Tuesday 4*th*, *August 1812*

Thick and foggy weather during these 24 hours. Variation per evening amplitude 24° 7′10″. Sounded in 45 fathoms on whale bank. All hands employed in necessary jobs.

No Observation

¶

22 days out *Wednesday 5*th*, *August 1812*

First part strong breezes and foggy weather. Under single-reefed foretopsail and foresail. Middle and latter part thick and cloudy with light winds inclining to calm. At 6 P.M. sent up fore-top gallant yard, fore-royal yard and mast and maintopmast. Let out all reefs. No soundings in 100 fathoms. 5 persons on the surgeon's list. Course E. by S. Wind W.

Variation 1 ¾ points westerly.

Latitude Observation 42° 59′

¶

Commences with calms and cloudy weather.

☞ At 4 P.M. the officers and company were summoned
aft to attend a court-martial held by the commander for
the trial of Benjamin W. Robbins, captain of marines, and
Nicholos Hinoff, one of his marines of the first division.
Great order, regularity and decorum were observed by all
persons during the trials. Captain Robbins was first im-
peached for having on the day of the battle with the *Royal
Bounty* neglected his duty, skulked below during the
greater part of the said action, and showing himself to be
a COWARD. The surgeon, gunner, gunner's mate, W. Moore
and Lieutenant Jones were duly sworn and examined touch-
ing these charges, and also several witnesses on behalf of
the accused. After hearing the defendants plea and a mature
consideration of all the evidence, the commander delivered
the following address and opinion of the court-martial—
"Captain Robbins, I do not approve of your conduct during the battle, you certainly neglected your duty as an
officer on board my vessel; you had no right to quit your
station in search of cartridges, but should have sent one of
your officers or marines upon that duty; and further when
you went below you ought instantly to have returned on
deck, whereas it appears you remained in the cabin assist-
ing the gunner in making cartridges for the great guns
(though he several times advised you to go on deck) till

the action was over: in fact the whole of your conduct appears to me and the other members of the court-martial to have been at least WRONG, and we are all of opinion that your late behavior shall be now overlooked, but should you hereafter be guilty of the like misconduct you shall forfeit all your prize money and be punished as the law directs." Nicholas Hinoff was then convicted of skulking behind the long-boat during the action, for which he was severely reprimanded and ordered to behave better for the future.

At ½ past 9 Isaac Butler saw a sail from aloft bearing S.E. upon the weather bow. Got out all the sweeps in chase. At Meridian still in chase of a vessel about 3 leagues upon the weather bow.

Latitude Observation 42° 19'

¶

24 days out   *Friday 7ᵗʰ, August 1812*

At 1 P.M. Richard Raven discovered a sail two points on the weather bow. At 2 came up with the sail we were in chase of yesterday, fired the bow gun, upon which the sail hoisted American colours and bore away under our lee. Hailed her and found her to be the American ship *Eliza-Ann*, Captain Eldridge of Boston from Liverpool bound to Baltimore with a full cargo of English drygoods. Sent Lieutenant Sweet on board with orders to send the captain and his papers on board the *Yankee*. Upon examining the captain and his papers it appeared that the cargo consisted entirely of English goods shipped by British merchants, consigned to ——— merchants in Baltimore, contrary to the non-importation act; that the property was insured in England and further that the shippers had obtained a regular license from their government protecting them against British capture, which License was to be forwarded by the first opportunity. For the above reasons the commander and officers considered the *Elisa-Ann* and her cargo as good and lawful prize, and sent Mr. Seth Barton as prize-master with a quartermaster with eight seamen on board (leaving Captain Eldridge and one boy) with a commission, instrucions, the ships papers sealed and directed to the owners together with several letters, giving them a full account of our cruise. The first and second mates with 8 seamen voluntarily entered on board the *Yankee* and signed the Articles. Captain Eldgidge informed us, that on the 1st August in Latitude 44° he passed through a fleet (90 sail in number) of British merchantmen 17 days out from Tortola bound home convoyed by a sloop of war. The sloop of war said that he had lost a number of his fleet in fogs, that they were all heavy ladened and many of them dull sailers. Day before yesterday Captain Eldridge saw a large black ship standing E. by N. and this morning passed another sail steering the same course. Captain Eldrige judged himself in Longitude 52°, as he got soundings on the bank yesterday and caught a number of fish.

☞ When all hands were piped to quarters, three of the invalids, Mason (who was wounded in the action with the *Royal Bounty*), Phillips and Asky took their stations. At daylight this morning discovered the sail ahead which we chased last night distant about 4 leagues. At ½ past 8 Andrew Tar saw a sail under the lee. At 10 P.M. spoke the Portuguese ship *Tentacao* from Philadelphia with rice, flour and corn, 16 days out, bound to Oporto. On Saturday she fell in with the British sloop of war *Mary-Ann* and on Sunday spoke an English privateer schooner from St. John's with six American prizes in company. At meridian two sails in sight. All sails set in chase. Light winds, smooth sea and pleasant weather.

4 persons on the Surgeon's list

Latitude Observation 41° 55′

¶

25 days out   *Saturday 8ᵗʰ, August 1812*

At 2 P.M. six sail in sight to the windward. Set all sail in chase of a brig ahead. At sundown discovered said brig to be a man of war, and hauled close upon the wind in pursuit of the sails to the windward, believing them to be her prizes. At day-light saw the fleet bearing N.W. Set sail in chase. At 10 P.M. several of the strange sails, distant about 2 leagues, hove to, made signals, and three of them, apparently large frigates, made all sail in chase of us; two of them standing close upon the wind to the eastward and the other to the southward. Luffed up close upon a wind and set all drawing sails: got in our leeward guns, shifted the shot boxes aft, trimmed the sails and prepared every thing for a race. At ¼ before 12 the two frigates fired several guns to the leeward, hoisted American colours and bore away to the westward. We supposed these frigates to be part of the American squadron, Commodore Rodgers, with several prizes in company bound home. The chase lasted nearly two hours; at first the easternmost frigate forelayed us and seemed to near us; but as soon as we had trimmed the brig by stationing all the men amidships, we plainly left her astern and she gave over the chase. Thus we have outsailed on a fair chase the swiftest frigate (no doubt the *President*) in the American Navy, and she is allowed to be as good a sailer as any in the British Navy.

Latitude Observation 41° 40′

¶

26 days out   *Sunday 9ᵗʰ, August 1812*

Commences with fresh breezes and rainy weather. At 10 P.M. single reefed mainsail and foretopsail. At 11 took in the fore and aft foresail. At 6 let out reefs and set sail. Course S.S.E. Wind variable. At ½ past 11 gibed ship to the N.E. 5 knots. At meridian squally with rain. Took in light sails. 9 knots. No sail in sight. 5 on the surgeon's list.

Latitude Observation 41° 29′

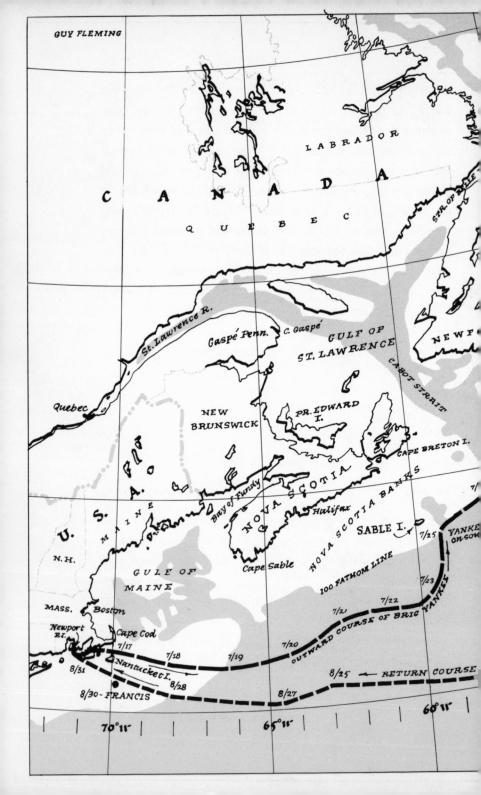

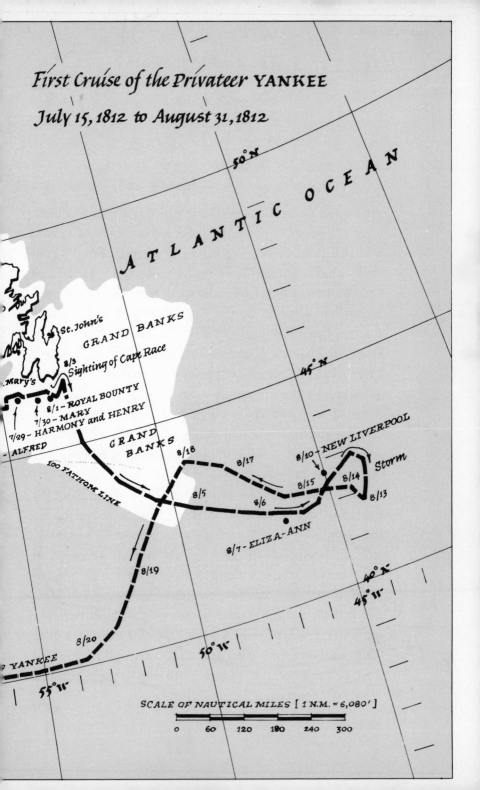

First Cruise of the Privateer YANKEE

July 15, 1812 to August 31, 1812

ATLANTIC OCEAN

50° N

45° N

40° N

St. John's

GRAND BANKS

8/3 Sighting of Cape Race

.Mary's

8/1 - ROYAL BOUNTY

7/30 - MARY

7/29 - HARMONY and HENRY

- ALFRED

GRAND BANKS

100 FATHOM LINE

8/18

8/17

8/10 - NEW LIVERPOOL

Storm

8/15

8/14

8/5

8/6

8/13

8/7 - ELIZA-ANN

8/19

45° W

8/20

50° W

40° N

YANKEE

55° W

SCALE OF NAUTICAL MILES [1 N.M. = 6,080']

0   60   120   180   240   300

¶

27 days out *Monday 10th, August 1812*

At 20 past 2 P.M. Lenas Wilding called out from masthead a sail 1 ½ points on the lee bow. Set sail in chase. At 4 called all hands to quarters and prepared for action. Fired 2 guns upon which the vessel hove to. At 5 run under her lee and ordered her to lower her colours, which she did immediately. Found her to be the English brig *New Liverpool*, Captain James Ritchie, 151 85/94 tons burthen, from Palma Island of Majorca, bound to Quebec, 35 days out with a cargo of 263 hogsheads, 116 pipes and 6 barrels of Benicalo (Valencia) red wine and 75 quintals Majorca Rosas Cork, invoiced at 27,189 dollars. The *New Liverpool* mounts 4 carriage guns and is only 3 years old and was navigated by 9 persons. This prize and her cargo may be reasonably estimated at $38,000.

At 9 P.M. fresh gales and flying clouds. Took in all the light sails. Sent down royal and topgallant masts and housed the masts. At 3 double reefed the foretopsail and mainsail, took the bonnet off the fore and aft foresail. At 4 took in the mainsail. At 5 sent down maintopgallant mast, clewed up the foretop sail and hove to under the fore and aft foresail. Middle and latter part strong gales, cloudy weather and a heavy sea. Shipped a great deal of water upon deck while scudding. At 7 A.M. saw a sail astern gibed ship and stood towards her. At 11 again gibed ship to the northward

and set the three-reefed mainsail, double reefed foretopsail, staysail and gib. Caught a large shark. At meridian
spoke the American brig *Hazard* of Boston from Lisbon
with salt bound home. The gale still continues with squalls
and rain.

No Observation

¶

28 days out   *Tuesday 11th, August 1812*

First part strong gales and cloudy with a heavy sea. At
6 P.M. Prince Wilding saw a sail from aloft bearing 2 points
on the lee bow. At 9 same man saw another sail bearing
due N. Sent up gallant masts and yards and set sail in chase
of the first mentioned vessel. At 11 being nearly calm got
out our sweeps and fired a gun upon which the sail hove to.
Sent the boat with Lieutenants Sweet and Jones on board.
Found her to be the American brig *Rebecca* of Boston from
London bound home with a full cargo of English drygoods
protected by a British license. Took possession of said brig
and ordered her into Bristol, when the captain showed us
his commission from Commodore Barney as a prize-master
of the said brig and stated that she was captured by the
[here the page is torn] privateer of Baltimore [here the
page is torn] Commodore Barney, mounting ten twelve
pounders with 130 men. Captain Abbott informed us that

on the 9th August he spoke a West India homeward bound fleet of 50 sail convoyed by the *Thetis* frigate Captain Bryan; that on the same day he was boarded by an officer from the *Guerriere* frigate and permitted to pass under the British License. The officer informed Captain Abbott that he had captured and burnt 20 sail of American merchantmen among others the *Concordia* of Marblehead whose Captain and crew, 12 in number, he put on board the *Rebecca*. Captain Abbott further mentioned that on the 7th August he spoke 2 English brigs from Lisbon bound to Quebec, steering to the northward, and also that the *Roscia* had captured and burnt 15 sail of fishermen on the bank and had sent in one English brig from Greenock with goods and an armed ship from Lisbon with salt after receiving one broadside. Permitted the *Rebecca* to proceed.

Latitude 43° 44'

¶

29 days out   *Wednesday 12ᵗʰ, August 1812*

At 2 P.M. appearances of squally weather took in topgallant sail staysails and gib. In chase of an English ship to the windward. Suddenly a violent squall struck us and hove us nearly upon our beam ends. Let fly the main halyards, topsail halyards and foresheet. Put the helm hard a lee. Handed the topsail and mainsail. Sent down the foretop gallant mast and yards. Also the maintopmast and rigged in the gib-boon. The storm increasing brailed up the fore and aft fore-sail—several tremendous squalls kept the vessel before them under the fore-stay-sail. The sea during these squalls made a fair breach over us. The water was frequently 3 feet deep upon our deck. Battened down the hatches fore and aft—struck the foretopmast, secured all the rigging in the top, lowered down the foreyard and made a span for the drag. The storm now increased to a perfect hurricane. The wind shifting to every point of the compass and in "taking the ruffian billows by the tops, curling their monstrous heads and hanging them with deafning clamour in the slippery shrouds." It was now thought adviseable to throw some of our guns overboard: accordingly we launched into the ocean the long nine and two six pounders, got all the shot boxes below into the cabin and stationed several men with axes ready to cut away the masts. The wind and sea both increasing, the commander ordered the vessel to be hove to. We therefore immediately prepared a drag by attaching the stream anchor to one of the cables, made several spars fast to it and fastened it round the mainmast and threw it over the weather quarter. Finding that the drag did not bring her bows sufficiently to the sea, we rigged and set one of the staysails to the mainmast. The vessel still la-boured excessively, the comins of the sea continually break-ing over her. Took the bonnet off the fore and aft foresail double reefed and set it. She now rode tolerable easy but shipped a great deal of water. The storm continued with great violence with a most dangerous sea, during the night and the latter part of these 24 hours.

Latitude 43° 12'

¶

30 days out   *Thursday 13ᵗʰ, August 1812*

During the whole of these 24 hours a heavy storm with violent squalls, some rain, and a very high sea. Laid the vessel to under the same sail as yesterday. Shipped a great deal of water. No sail in sight. 13 persons on the surgeon's list, mostly with bad colds.

Latitude Observation 41° 58′ — Longitude Lunar
Observation 44′
Winds N.W. Course S.W.

¶

31 days out   *Friday 14ᵗʰ, August 1812*

The day commences with strong gales, flying clouds and a heavy sea. At meridian tacked ship to the northward and set the three-reefed mainsail. At 8 P.M. the weather moderated, let out all the reefs and set the jib and foretopsail. At 9 sent up foretopgallant mast and yard. Got three guns out of the hold instead of those we threw overboard. Opened all the hatches, got all the baggage upon deck and cleaned out ship fore and aft. Repaired the boat, set the old mainsail having split the leach of the new one at 10 last night. Middle and latter part of these 24 hours pleasant weather, clear sky, smooth sea and gentle breezes. Wind N. Course N.N.E. 3 on the surgeon's list.

Latitude Observation 42° 1′—Longitude Lunar 44° 00′

¶

32ᵈ day   *Saturday 15ᵗʰ, August 1812*

First and middle part squally with rain. Latter part fair and pleasant with light breezes from the N.E. Course W.N.W.
Latitude Observation 42° 25′

¶

33ᵈ day   *Sunday 16ᵗʰ, August 1812*

The day commences with fair weather, gentle breezes and a smooth sea. At 4 P.M. piped all hands to quarters, stationed the men at their respective guns and exercised them with loading and firing by divisions and giving the enemy a broadside either from the starboard or laboured side. Trained the marines and officers with muskets to the necessary maneuvers on board an armed vessel; vis in loading and firing with great expedition, in aiming at the enemy or their port holes; in forming themselves either on the bows, amidships, to the windward or leeward; in securing themselves by falling on the right knee loading, rising and firing. They then went through the manual exercise. The commander was highly gratified in observing the improvement of the whole company in their discipline, and said he would not hesitate with such fine fellows to lay along side of any letter-of-marque or vessel of equal force in the British service.

Saturday night. Being a fine pleasant moonlight evening the officers and company amused themselves with music dancing and singing. The commander and officers were greatly amused in noting the spirit and vivacity of the *Yankee's* crew. Every individual indeed seemed to partake of the pleasures of music and the "masy dance." The surgeon in particular displayed great activity in his riggadoons, sachés and pigeon-wings and excited infinite merriment by his somersaults and feats of tumbling. Joy and satisfaction sparkled in every eye while they drank "a good health to all sweethearts and wives." In fine the whole evening was devoted to amusement, fun and laughter.

Middle part nearly calm. Latter part fresh breeses from the S.S.E. Course N. by E. 7 knots. No sail in sight. Invalids all returned to duty, except Chace who improves daily.

Latitude Observation 43° 24'

¶

34 days out   *Monday 17ᵗʰ, August 1812*

At 1 P.M. Nathanael Peirce discovered a sail bearing 4
points on the lee bow. Set sail in chase. At 5 spoke the fine
new American ship *Minerva Smith*, Captain Charles Mann,
from Gottenburg 42 days out from Kiel bound to Philadelphia—with a cargo of sundries, ballast & 47 passengers
(30 ladies). Captain Mann informed us that 14 days ago
he was boarded by the convoy of the West India Fleet of
90 sail, who informed him of the war and oredered him to
follow the commodore. That during the succeeding night
it being squally and very dark he up helm and left the fleet.
They had one American schooner in company as a prize.
Captain M. has spoke no other vessels and brings no particular news. Longitude per *Minerva* 48°. Permitted her to
proceed. First part fresh breeses and pleasant weather. Middle part squally with heavy rain and a heavy sea. Sent down
yards and masts as usual. Took in all sail except the fore
and aft foresail and fore-staysail and lay to, the wind at
N.E.; wet cold and dark. At 8 A.M. the weather moderated
but still cloudy with occasional squalls. At 9 saw a sail to
windward. Set the mainsail fortopsail, gib, squareforesail
and staysails in chace. At meridian the sail still in view
about 4 miles to windward.

Latitude Observation 43° 39′

Chace, Askey, Robbins, and Dr. Wheaton on the sick list.

¶

35ᵗʰ day   *Tuesday 18ᵗʰ, August 1812*

During the whole of these 24 hours frequent squalls with rain and fogs. The sail we chased yesterday was found to be the *Minerva Smith*. Wind N.W. Course W.S.W. At 35 minutes past 11 A.M., the fog breaking away, discoverd six men of war to windward distant about 4 leagues. Immediately set all our sails and kept away S. by W. 10 knots per log. At meridian 3 of the sails, 2 ships, and a Brig in chase of us with all their canvas out.

No Observation

¶

36 days out   *Wednesday 19ᵗʰ, August 1812*

At meridian the men of war still in chase of us under full sail distant about 4 leagues, and the other two luffing up in pursuit of the Ship Minerva. Wind N.W. by N. Course S.S.W. Fresh breezes and thick weather. Set fore-royal, studdingsails, and ring-tale. 10 knots per log. At 3 P.M., the wind increasing with a considerable swell, one of the frigates seemed to forelay and near us, upon which we started seven puncheons of water and trimmed the vessel by stationing all hands aft. At 4 the frigate showed Ameri-

can colours and we hoisted ours at the main peak. At 5
fired a gun to leeward, which was immediately answered
by the frigate in the same manner. She now bore N. ½ W.
distant about 3 leagues; the wind and sea both increasing
and favouring her. At 6 she hoisted an American Jack at
her fore-royalmast head. At sundown she bore N. by W.
distant about 5 miles. From 9 to 10 she fired several shot
which fell short of us. We now prepared to serve our
enemy a Yankee trick by filling a cask with combustibles
and shot of various kinds, setting it on fire and lowering it
down from the lee quarter. Shortly after we observed a
very warm engagement between the frigate and our old
tar barrel; by the light of which we fortunately made our
escape. At 11 the frigate showed a blue light as a signal
and gave up the chase, which had lasted near 12 hours.

It being squally with rain took in all light sails, sent
down yards and topgallantmasts and hawled up W. by N.
under easy sail.

Middle part nearly calm. Latter part light winds and
hazy. Two persons on the Surgeon's List.

Latitude Observation 40° 55′

¶

37ᵗʰ day   *Wednesday 20ᵗʰ, August 1812*

Commences with gentle breezes and cloudy weather. At
3 P.M. discovered a sail ahead. Set all sail in chase. At 4 the

haze breaking away saw a large armed ship close under the lee, supposing her to be an English frigate instantly took in studding-sails and luffed up close upon the wind. At ½ past 4 the ship being abeam hoisted a red signal at her main-top; upon which we fired a gun to leeward and showed English colours. At 5 tacked ship to the southward in pursuit of her. At ½ past 5 being distant about 2 miles observed the sail to be a large straight frigate built English ship, showing eleven guns upon a side, with high bulwarks and apparently full of men. Believing her to be a British packet from [the] Bermudas and Halifax bound home without a cargo, the commander consulted with his officers and company, and after mature deliberation it was thought prudent to give over the chase, which was done accordingly. At sundown fresh gales and dark cloudy weather. Took in all light sails and sent down royal yard and mast. Wind N. Course W.N.W.—7 knots. During the night heavy squalls, dark and cloudy, with rain and a high sea, frequently breaking over the vessel. Close upon the wind under double-reefed foretopsail, three-reefed mainsail and foretopmast staysail.

At daylight this morning discovered 5 men of war upon our weather quarter, distant about 10 miles. It blowing strong with a heavy sea, we were able only to carry top-gallant sail. At 7 finding that one of the frigates evidently came up with us notwithstanding all the sail we could carry, it was considered a necessary measure to lighten our vessel. We therefore threw four of our fore-lee bow guns overboard. At ½ past 7 we hoisted American colours, which the frigate answered in the same manner, hauled up close upon a wind and gave over the chase. We now knew them to be the American squadron, Commodore Rogers. This is the third time we have been chased by the *American squadron*.

Latter part strong gales and a heavy sea with cloudy weather.

Latitude Observation 40° 10′

¶

38ᵗʰ day   *August 21ˢᵗ, 1812*

First part gentle breezes and a clear sky. Wind N. by E. Course W. by N. ½ N. 7 knots.

Middle part light airs and pleasant weather. Sent up foretopgallant yard and set the sail.

Latter part rainy with sudden squalls. Took in all light sails and sent down royal and yard and mast. At ½ past 11 lowered down the mainsail, clewed up the topsail, took in square and fore and aft foresail. At meridian strong appearances of squally weather with numerous waterspouts to the windward.

Latitude Observation 40° 10′ — Varn. 20° West

¶

39ᵗʰ day   *August 22ᵈ, 1812*

First part frequent squalls with heavy rain. Saw a waterspout forming close upon the weather quarter, fired a
cannonball into it, upon which it dispersed. From 12 midnight till 4 A.M. strong gales, violent squalls, and a heavy sea.
Took in all light sails and scud before the wind under the
foretopmast staysail. Sent down topgallant yard and mast
and maintopmast; rigged in the gib boom; lowered down
the foreyard, got ever ready for a blow. At 9 A.M. the
weather moderated. Set sail accordingly; sent up fore yard
and topgallant mast. Fair and pleasant weather. Wind
E.N.E. Course W.N.W.

Latitude Observation 40° 22′

¶

40ᵗʰ day   *August 23ᵈ, 1812*

During these 24 hours cloudy weather with floods of rain
attended with violent squalls of wind and a heavy swell.
Wind N.W. Course W.N.W. Chace, Asky, Fornsberg,
and Robbins on the sick list.

Latitude Observation 40° 54′

¶

41ˢᵗ day   *August 24ᵗʰ, 1812*

First part strong breezes with a great swell.

Middle and latter part gentle gales and pleasant weather. Wind E. Course W.

No sail in sight—all hands employed about ship's duty. Peter Olney the carpenter broke his thumb while repairing the jolly boat. 2 persons on the surgeon's list.

Latitude Observation 40° 28′

¶

42ᵈ day   *August 25ᵗʰ, 1812*

Commences with light airs and pleasant weather. Under studding sails below and aloft. At 10 P.M. took in studding sails, fore-royal and staysails—sent down royal yard and mast. At 6 A.M. took in topgallant sail and single reefed the mainsail and foretopsail.

Latter part strong winds from the S.W. Cloudy weather. Course W. by N.

The evening being extremely pleasant, the crew amused themselves with music, dancing, and singing.

Longitude per lunar Observation 63° 3′ 45″

Latitude Observation 40° 46′ N.
Chace is the only invalid.

¶

43ᵈ day   *August 26ᵗʰ, 1812*

During the greater part of these 24 hours squally weather
with heavy rain. Wind variable. Nothing remarkable.
Latitude Observation 40° 38′

¶

44ᵗʰ day   *August 27ᵗʰ, 1812*

Commences with rainy weather and frequent squalls. Made
and took in sail accordingly. At 6 P.M. discovered a sail on
the weather bow standing to the N.E. distant about ½ a
league. Luffed up and let reefs out of mainsail and topsail.
Set the gib the square and fore and aft foresail, upon which
the sail tacked to the W. under her mainsail foresail and
gib. During the chase several heavy squalls with floods of
rain frequently made and took in sail as occasion required.
At 7, being within gun shot of the sail, fired several shot
at her. Still showing no colours, we gave her a broadside,
when she tacked ship to the N.E. We gave her another

broadside as she passed us and tacked ship in pursuit of her. Shortly after it commenced blowing with great violence. Took in gib square foresail and mainsail. At 8, being extremely dark with torrents of rain and blowing a strong gale from the E., lost sight of the sail. The commander therefore thought proper to give over the chase and stand upon our course to the W. The sail we chased appeared to be a long handsome pilot-boat built schooner and we are inclined to think she was a Bermudas privateer.

At 9 the gale increasing took in all sail except foretopmast and staysail and foresail and scud before it. Sent down topgallant yard and mast, also maintopmast and fore yard. At 12 midnight the weather moderated. We set the lower sails. At sunrise, being pleasant weather, sent up yards and masts and set all sail.

Latter part clear sky with a smooth sea, nearly calm. All hands employed in customary duty.

Latitude Observation 40° 8'

Longitude Lunar Observation 64° 15'

Chace improves in health daily.

¶

45th day   *August 28th, 1812*

At 4 P.M. saw a sail ahead. Set all sail in chase. Hazy weather with a smooth sea and the wind from the N. At

9 P.M. came up with the sail [and] fired a shot under her stern, upon which she hove to. Found her to be the schooner *Ann & Mary*, Robert Avery, master, 53 days out from Cadiz bound to New London in ballast. Captain Avery saw a sail at sundown from his foreyard bearing N.W., and 10 days ago spoke an American brig from London bound to Baltimore, who informed him of the War.

Middle part flying clouds and appearance of squally weather—run under easy sail. At sunrise saw five sails from mast-head, three of them to the northward and two the southward all standing to the westward. Supposing them to be Americans bound into Boston Bay the commander did not think it advisable to chase them. At 9 A.M. rounded to and sounded—found bottom in 83 fathoms with green ore. Set studding sails aloft and below, also staysails and flying gib. At meridian sounded in 45 fathoms white and black sand—very pleasant. Wind N. and N.E. Course W. by N. a small sail in sight.

Latitude Observation 40° 26′ — Longitude Observation 48° 4′ 30″

¶

August 29ᵗʰ, 1812

This day begins with very pleasant weather with gentle gales and a smooth sea. At ½ past 12 Prince Wilding discovered a sail three points on the weather bow distant about 5 leagues. At sundown the sail bore W. by S. distant about 2½ leagues; all sails set in chase. At 11 P.M. boarded the American ship *Frances* of New Orleans from Greenock bound to New York with a full cargo of English drygoods protected by a British license. After examining her papers, detained her as a good and lawful prize on the following grounds, namely, 1st, because she sails under a British license in time of War; 2d, because her cargo consists entirely of British manufactured goods; 3d, Because she loaded and sailed from England after the declaration of war was received; 4th, because the cargo is consigned to order with written instruction to proceed to Halifax and there deliver the cargo in case the non-importation act should not be taken off; 5th, because said ship intended to violate the non-importation law, and lastly, because all the above reasons plainly show the said cargo to be bona fide British property. Sent Mr. Prince Eldridge on board commissioned as prize master with orders to keep company with the brig and follow her into port. The ship's paper were sealed and put in his possession. Captain Boyer informed us that eight days ago he was boarded by an office from the *Jason* frigate, Captain Deane, who mentioned that he had captured several American vessels and sent them in, that the United States vessel of war *Nautilus* had been taken by a British frigate, that he had heard at Halifax that a battle had been fought between the American and British troops on the lines, that the former were defeated with the loss of 700 men. Captain Boyer further informed us that he had been boarded by a British lugger, the captain of which told him that a few days before he had been fired into by a large armed vessel and that he escaped into the fog. Captain Boyer, when off the south tale of the Great Bank, saw an engagement between an American frigate and the convoy of the *West India*. Homeward bound fleet of 180 sail, the battle seemed to be very warmly contested and when he lost sight of them they were still engaged.

The Declaration of War was received in England with great murmurs and disapprobation, the people were highly dissatisfied with their rulers and were ripe for mutiny and insurrection. It was supposed that a revolution was inevitable.

The captain of the *Frances* estimated his cargo at $500,000.

Middle and latter part pleasant gales and fine weather. Course N.W.

All hands employed about ship's duty.

Chace (our poor invalid), being much better, was assisted on deck and is now in a fair way to recover.

At 10 A.M. the South Shoal bore N.W. and N. distant 48 miles.

Latitude Observation 40° 29′

¶

August 30ᵗʰ, 1812

Commences with gentle breezes and a smooth sea. A sail in sight from most head just visible to the leeward. Middle part very pleasant. Wind S.W. by W. Course N.W.

by W. Soundings in 27 fathoms at 8 P.M. At 5 A.M. the man at mast head called out, "Land under the lee." At 6 A.M. saw Noman's Land & Gay Head Light bearing N. At 7 discovered a sail standing in for the land. At 8 saw point Judith Light distant about 4 leagues. At 9 saw Rhode Island Light—spoke a sloop bound to Nantucket who informed us that Fort Wolcott on the frontiers had been taken by the Americans. The *Francis* in company. At meridian Rhode Island Light bears N.W. by N. distant 2 miles.

¶

Sunday 31ˢᵗ, August 1812

At 1 P.M. passed Fort Wolcott and fired a salute of 7 guns, which was answered from the fort. At 2 arrived in Bristol Harbour and gave them a royal (or more properly, a loyal) salute of 7 guns. We then came to anchor and clewed up all sails and went on shore where we were received with three cheers by the friendly inhabitants of Bristol, which was returned by the *Yankee's* crew. On enquiry found, that the *Henry* had arrived at Bristol, the *Harmony* at New York, and the *Eliza Ann* at Boston. The *New Liverpool* is the only prize nor arrived.

Thus ends this journal.

¶ ¶

¶

District and Port of Bristol, October 13ᵗʰ, 1812

I, OLIVER WILSON, commander of the brig *Yankee*, do solemnly swear that the foregoing is a true journal of the late course of said brig and that all the material occurrences on the course are therein faithfully recorded.

So help me God.

Oliver Wilson

SWORN TO BEFORE

Charles Collins

District and Port of Bristol, October 13th
1812–

I Oliver Wilson Commander of the Brig
Yankee, do solemnly swear that the foregoing
is a true Journal of the late cruise of said
Brig and that all the material occurrences
on the cruise are therein faithfully recorded
So help me God– *Oliver Wilson*

Sworn to before
Chas Collins Coll'r

*Captain Oliver Wilson's sworn statement
that the events described in the first
journal are "faithfully recorded"*

¶ ¶

¶

I, JAMES RITCHIE, late master of the English brig *New Liverpool*, captured on the 10ᵗʰ ultimate by the brig of war *Yankee*, Wilson commander, and myself and crew brought into this port as prisoners of war, do hereby promise and declare that I will still consider myself as a prisoner of war on parole and liable to be exchanged as such when an exchange of prisoners shall take place; and further that I am ready to obey the officers authorized to dispose of prisoners of war.

James Ritchie

Bristol, Rhode Island
2 September, 1812

I James Ritchie late
Master of the English Brig New
Liverpool captured on the 10th ult.
by the Brig of War Yankee Wilson
Commander and myself been
Bought into this port as Prisoners
of War; Ao hereby promise & declare
that I will still consider myself
as a Prisoner of War on parole
& liable to be exchanged as such
when an exchange of prisoners
shall take place; and further
that I am ready to obey the Officers
authorized to dispose of Prisoners of War
Bristol R. I.—   James Ritchie
2 Sep. 1812

Letter from the prisoner James Ritchie
promising good behavior while
aboard the Yankee

Journal

OF THE SECOND CRUISE

❁

Commencing October 17th, 1812

Journal

on board

The Private Armed Brig

Yankee,

Oliver Wilson

Commander,

During her 2d Cruise.

By A Wanderer.

1812.

Title page of the second journal

The Second Cruise

Art thou a Wanderer?—hast thou seen
O'erwhelming tempests drown thy bark?
A shipwreck's sufferer hast thou been,
    Misfortune's mark?

Tho' long of winds and waves the sport,
Condemn'd in wretchedness to roam,
LIVE!—thou shalt reach a sheltering port,
    A quiet home.
                —MONTGOMERY

My fortune leads to traverse realms alone
And find no spot of all the earth my own.
                —GOLDSMITH

    Multosque per annos
Erabit acti fatis maria omnia circum.
                —VIRGIL

¶ ¶

¶

Saturday 17ᵗʰ, October 1812

It is the nature of man to be fond of novelty and variety.
At least I have found my nature to be such. For I had not
remained at home a month from our last cruise before I
became anxious to take another. My health, which is always
indifferent on shore, grew daily worse; my spirits became
depressed; I observed daily accounts in the newspapers of
numerous valuable prizes captured both by our public and
private armed vessels and detailed statements of several
gallant achievements by the officers and companys of such
vessels: all these objects and motives combined in urging
me again to sea. The *Yankee* was preparing for a second
cruise. I knew her captain well and esteemed him much.
He invited me to take the command of the marines and
again to act as his clerk, or, more properly, as purser of
the vessel. Why should I refuse this invitation? What could
I do on shore? Winter was coming on; the cold blast of
January would little agree with my feeble constitution; my
prize-money for the last cruise was not yet received, and
moreover it was extremely doubtful whether our prizes
would net us anything considerable. Under those circumstances would it be prudent, would it be adviseable in any
light to remain at home? Surely not. The owners of the

Yankee also wished me to go out in her again. I had kept the *Yankee's* books; regulated her accounts; calculated the shares; paid the officers and seamen; made out articles, powers of attorney, letters, documents, etc. In fact, without vanity, my services had been of the greatest consequences to them and they expected I would go in her again. Therefore I resolved to take a second trip in the *Yankee*. I made all the necessary preparations and fortified my mind against the dangers and difficulties of a six month's cruise.

Our prospects are certainly very flattering. We have an excellent little vessel that sails remarkably fast; mounts seventeen guns and is manned with one hundred as prime lads as ever went to sea. Our officers are all young, active, enterprising men; fearless of danger and thirsting for Fortune and Glory.

Our commander, Oliver Wilson, is a native of Connecticut, about 27 years of age, has been accustomed to the seas from his earliest years, and is every inch a sailor. Nursed and formed, as it were, amidst the hardships and perils of a seafaring life, he knows every part of a seaman's duty. Dire necessity taught him the discipline of the British navy. He was pressed [impressed] and for several years compelled to serve His Majesty. By this means he became an able disciplinarian. As a man Captain Wilson is cheerful, generous, candid, fond of his friends and companions, but despises the fopperies of fashionable life. He respects and admires the female sex, but custom has rendered their society less pleasing to him than to those who continually bask in the sunshine of beauty's smile.

O'er our gay vessel and her daring band,
Experienc'd Wilson holds the chief command;
Tho' train'd in boisterous elements, he's mind
To yet by soft humanity refin'd
Abroad confest the father of his crew!
Brave, liberal, just.

Lieutenant Barton, our first officer, is an honest, good-hearted, brave fellow; his manners are plain, blunt, unassuming. He was early bred to the sea, has made several voyages around the world, was formerly engaged in the north west American trade; escaped from numerous perils both on land and at sea; was once taken prisoner by the savages and sold; on another occasion his captain and the greater part of the crew were murdered on their own decks. Barton and three others rushed upon deck from the forecastle armed with knives, occasioned a great slaughter among the savages, and drove them overboard into the sea. In fact Lieutenant Barton is a complete son of Neptune, fond of a seaman's character and inured to all the perils of the ocean.

Such Barton is, by learning unrefin'd
That oft enlightens to corrupt the mind.
Boisterous of manners; train'd in early youth
To scenes that shame the conscious cheek of truth.
In art unschool'd, each veteran rule he priz'd
And all improvement haughtily despis'd.
Yet tho' full oft to future perils blind,
With skill superior glow'd his daring mind,

Thro' scenes of death the reeling bark to guide,
When midnight shades involve the raging tide.

The second lieutenant, John H. Vinson of Newport, is
apparently a man of affable pleasing manners, of a quick
temper, moderate capacity, amazingly attached to the female sex, careless of the present or the future, vain of his
person and dress, anxious to distinguish himself merely to
be spoken of, but by no means daring or venturesome. He
is not a sailor by profession, but was brought up behind the
counter. In a word he is a man who will never rise above
mediocrity but may sink much below it.

Thomas Jones, our third lieutenant, is of a very different
character from the other two—gay, thoughtless, dissipated;
fond of pleasure, wine, and women; careless of the gifts of
fortune; negligent of the opinion of the world, acting according to the impulse of the moment; respectful to strangers, but improperly familiar with his acquaintances. He is
said to be a tolerable sailor, yet he wants prudence. I believe him to be brave because thoughtless, and venturesome
because inconsiderate. He is a man whom everyone may
like but no one either respects or admires.

Our sailing-master, Elisha Snow, is a compound of different qualifications. On shore his manners are tolerably
genteel, he visits in good society, is pleased with feminine
accomplishments, anxious to become a husband and a
father, wishing to please but seldom succeeding; of a person
masculine and tolerably handsome, but his mind by no
means refined by learning and science. At sea he is rough,
unaccommodating, extremely attached to his own opinion,

courageous without judgment and assuming without experimental knowledge; for he was not always a sailor. As a navigator I believe him to be tolerably correct; he calculates the longitude, takes lunars, observes the stars, and makes the inferior officers and seamen wonder at his superior knowledge.

> Him science taught by mystic lore to trace
> The planets wheeling in eternal race;
> To mark the ship in floating balance held
> By earth attracted and by seas repell'd,
> Or point her devious track thro' climes unknown,
> That leads to every shore and every zone.

What shall I say of our surgeon Dr. Miller? He is a man of such uniformity of character that it is difficult to describe him in particular terms. However, he appears to be a young man of common natural talents with considerable knowledge of surgery acquired from his brother; by no means a classic scholar or well read; almost entirely ignorant of the world and its multifareous manners, as he has always resided in a village, totally unacquainted with life and the duplicities of the human heart, credulous of what he hears and filled with astonishment at every novel object. His manners are modest but rather particular, quite complacent, and never offensive. He is one who may be generally liked but never loved. His chief passion seems to be, as is the case with most of his profession, the love of money. At present I neither like nor dislike Dr. Miller. Time will prove whether he is worthy of my friendship.

At present the only person on board the *Yankee* whom I should wish to call by the sacred title of Friend is our captain. I know he has a good heart and a benevolent disposition; he has behaved towards me with peculiar kindness and I have every reason to esteem him. Were our opinions and manners more congenial no doubt we should be as intimate hereafter as we are at present.

Before I conclude this account of the *Yankee's* officers, it may be expected that I should mention the purser and captain of marines. And yet why is it necessary to record a name and character so little known to Fame and Fortune?

> But what avails it to record a name,
> That counts no rank among the sons of fame?
> While yet a stripling, oft with fond alarms,
> His bosom danc'd to nature's boundless charms.
> On him fair science dawn'd, in happier hour,
> Awakening into bloom young fancy's flower,
> But frowning fortune with untimely blast,
> The blossom wither'd, and the dawn o'ercast,
> Forlorn of heart and by severe decree,
> *Condemned reluctant to the faithless sea;*
> With long farewell he left the laurel grove,
> Where science and the tuneful sisters rove.
> Hither he wandered, anxious to explore
> Antiquities of nations now no more,
> To penetrate each distant realm unknown
> And range excursive o'er th' untravel'd zone.
> In vain! for rude adversity's command,

Still on the margin of each famous land,
With unrelenting ire his steps oppos'd
And every gate of Hope against him clos'd.

Shall we endeavour to perpetuate the memory and calami-
ties of a man born to suffer all the pangs and arrows of out-
rageous fortune? Is there a person in existence who will
sympathize in the sufferings of a poor Wanderer? No wife,
no child, no favorite mistress to be interested in his fate,
who will shed the tear of compassion, or heave the sigh of
regret, if chance consigns him to the bosom of the deep
or disease leaves his bones to bleach on Africa's dreary
coast? Ah well.

Should fate command him to the farthest verge of the
green earth, to distant barbarous climes, where first the sun
gilds Indian mountains, or his setting beam flames on the
Atlantic isles?

Yet still will his heart beat responsive to the ties of
kindred affection and vibrate to all the softer passions of
the soul.

It was on Friday afternoon the 16th of October 1812,
that Captain Wilson, attended by his lieutenants, master
surgeon, and purser, repaired on board the *Yankee*: immediately all hands were piped to muster; the purser took
a list of all persons on board and we had exactly one hundred men. The ensuing evening was employed by the
officers in writing farewell letters to their relations and
friends. Horatio first wrote a letter to his honored mother,
bidding her an affectionate adieu, wishing her all the bless-
ings that heaven could bestow upon the virtuous and good,

thanking her for past kindnesses and enclosing a small present, being the only money he possessed in the world. He also wrote several other letters to his brothers and sisters, acknowledging the many obligations he had received from all of them and promising future remuneration should kind fortunes ever put it in his power.

On Saturday at daylight sailing orders were issued by the commander. Fired a gun, set the colours, and loosed the topsails. The boatswain piped all hands:

> Thrice with shrill note the Boatswain's whistle rung
> *All hands unmoor!* proclaims a boisterous cry:
> *All hands unmoor!* the cavern's rocks reply!

At 6 A.M. we got under way and stood out of Newport harbour with a fair wind. The sun was just rising from behind the hills, enlivening every object with his lucid beams. A great number of small vessels and boats were leaving port bound to sea upon their usual occupations; the martial music from the ports was beating the reveillie, and every surrounding object filled the mind with joy and satisfaction. As we passed the privateer *Tom* of Baltimore we gave them three cheers, which was returned by her whole crew consisting of 130 men. When opposite Fort Wolcott we fired a salute, set all drawing sails and at 7 A.M. left Newport Light astern. At 9 o'clock Block Island was just visible from the deck, from which we took our departure bound out to sea upon a most long and dangerous cruise. As we saw the land for the last time, each feeling heart swelled with anxiety, hope, and fear, and each tearful eye cast many

A long lingering look behind.

How many tender recollections rush upon the heart when we are about to leave our country, relations, and friends! How few are so callous and indifferent as not to own some kindred attachment? Horatio deeply felt all the emotions of the lover, friend, relation, and patriot. His bosom's lord beat high with a thousand soft emotions. He was about entering upon a perilous voyage, his health was extremely delicate, his mind but little calculated from education and habit to associate with the rude sons of Neptune; yet necessity compelled him to seek for Fortune and reputation even in the "cannon's mouth." He left many dear relations, several estimable friends, numerous agreeable acquaintances, and above all, a most lovely and amiable girl, to whom his heart was sincerely attached: add to these the thousand comforts and conveniences of domestic life—all these Horatio left to encounter storms and tempests, bloodshed and slaughter, perils and dangers without name or number. Farewell, ye tranquil pleasures of social life! I sacrifice ye all at the imperious calls of Fate and Fortune.

Adieu, ye pleasures of the rural scene,
Where peace and calm contentments dwell serene!
To me in vain, on earth's prolific soil,
With summer crown'd th' Elysian vallies smile!
To me those happier scenes no joy impart
But tantalize with hope my aching heart.
For these, alas! reluctant I forego!
To visit storms and elements of woe!
Ye tempests o'er my head congenial roll,

To suit the mornful music of my soul!
In black progression, lo! they hover near;
Hail social horrors, like any fate severe!
Old ocean hail, beneath whose azure zone,
The secret deep lies unexplor'd, unknown.

Scarce had we lost sight of the land when we saw several large ships under a press of sail standing towards us. We knew them to be the enemy's frigates. Immediately set all sail and hauled up close upon the wind. The weather was mild and pleasant with gentle breezes and a smooth sea; in such weather we feared nothing; we felt perfectly secure and had the whole British navy been under our lee, we must have escaped. In four hours we lost sight of them entirely. We now set all drawing sails and shaped our course for the Cape de Verds. It was agreed between the owners and our captain that he should first steer for the above mentioned islands, there obtain a supply of water and fresh provisions; then run down the coast of Africa, look in at all the different ports, capture all vessels which we might discover, steer for Cape St. Augustine, cruise there for vessels trading to Brazil, touch at various islands for supplies and water, and after manning out the greater part of our crew return home in the spring.

¶

2ᵈ day

This day commenced a furious gale, which lasted ten days.
The wind frequently changed and blew with great violence
from every point of the compass. We sometimes scud before
the furious storm and at other times lay to heading the
tempest. The sea rose to a mountainous height, the vessel
laboured excessively and was continually covered with
water. The *Yankee* being a small vessel and built for a fast-
sailer, taut-rigged, with heavy spars, and a great weight of
metal upon deck, was little calculated for comfort and
safety. For these reasons we suffered greatly from the seas
breaking over the vessel and penetrating every part of her.
The cabin, notwithstanding all our endeavours, was
drenched with water. Our clothes, bedding, trunks, etc.
were all as wet as if thrown into the sea. The cabin being
closed, the weather warm, the vessel tight, the bilge-water
became insufferably disgusting. Yet here amidst wet and
dirt and nauseas of every description we were obliged to
live, or more properly, to exist. Above the tempest roared,
the storm imperious howled, the lightnings played upon
the surface of the deep, the thunder shook the Atlantic
even to the center and all nature seemed convulsed with
agonizing woe. To render the scene still more dreadful it
was night, dark, gloomy, comfortless night.

Cimmerian darkness shades the deep around,
Save when the lightnings gleaming on the sight,
Flash thro' the gloom a pale disastrous light
Above all other, fraught with scenes of woe
With grim destruction threatening all below!
Beneath the storm-lash'd surges furious rise,
And wave uproll'd on wave, assails the skies:
With ever-floating bulwarks they surround
The ship, half-swallow'd in the black profound!
With ceaseless hazard and fatigue opprest,
Dismay and anguish every heart possest!

¶

3ᵈ day

The second watch had just called the hour of one, and
passed the word from all parts of the ship, that "All's well,"
when suddenly a furious squall of wind, thunder, lightning,
and rain struck our little vessel and almost capsized her.
Instantly the lieutenant of the watch ordered the seamen
to let fly sheets and halyards, clew and brail up the sails,
keep the helm hard a weather and scud the vessel before
the blast.

And see! in confluence borne before the blast.
Clouds roll'd on clouds the dusty night o'ercast.
The blackening ocean curls; the winds arise
And the dark scud in quick succession flies!

¶

4ᵗʰ day

At 5 P.M. we discovered two large sails astern in chase of
us. Instantly luffed up on a wind and set as much sail as
we could carry, it blowing a strong gale from the S.W.
8 o'clock at night lost sight of these sails. There can be
little doubt but these vessels were British men of war. Had
it not been near night they might have occasioned us much
trouble and anxiety, or perhaps terminated our cruise at
Halifax or [the] Bermudas. But good fortune seems to
hover over the *Yankee*; whenever danger or distress sur-
rounds her, nay, when destruction appears inevitable, some
lucky chance rescues her from impending fate and guides
her to safety and security.

¶

6ᵗʰ day

Spoke the American ship *Ariadne* of Boston, Captain Bart-
lett Holmes, from Alexandria, bound to Cadis, 17 days out.
Captain Holmes informed us, that on the 11th instant he
was boarded by an officer from the American frigate *United
States*, Commodore Decatur; that the *Ariadne's* crew hav-

ing mutinied he requested Commodore Decatur to take six
of the ringleaders on board the frigate, which he did accordingly. Captain Holmes also mentioned, that his ship
had sprung a leak during a heavy gale, that he was obliged
to keep both pumps going, that he was short handed, and
his crew still mutinous, for which reasons he was bound
home again in distress. Whilst on board the *Ariadne* our
lieutenant observed the disorderly conduct of her crew,
particularly of the cook, a stout Negro fellow, who not
only abused but stuck his captain and mate, and moreover
called our bargemen a set of pirates and villains. On being
informed of this circumstance Captain Wilson requested
permission of Captain Holmes (which was of course
granted) to punish said Negro as an example to the rest of
his crew. Accordingly Mr. Cuffy was tied to the windlass
and each of the boat's crew as well as the *Ariadne's* officers,
gave him a dozen to teach him his duty and good manners
in [the] future. The purser then wrote a letter to the owners, informing them of the good health and spirits of the
Yankee's company and her situation in Latitude 35°N. and
Longitude 56°W. Permitted the *Ariadne* to proceed.

¶

8ᵗʰ day

During the late heavy gales our ship suffered considerable
damage, having carried away three of her spars, stove the

arm-chests, injured the bulwarks, and strained the ship in every part. One of our prize-masters, an old seaman who had crossed the Atlantic upwards of thirty times, observed that he had often sailed *over* the Atlantic but never before sailed *under* it; for we had been literally covered with the waves of the ocean during the last eight days.

Whilst the storms, rain, and thunder lasted we observed a great variety of rainbows, frequently several at a time, and of the most brilliant colours. It is something remarkable, that when the seas roll mountainous high and break with violence against each other, that every spray forms a little rainbow, which appeared and vanished almost instantaneously. One evening, just after a heavy shower, when the dark clouds were settling towards the western horison and the full moon was rising in unclouded majesty, we discovered a beautiful lunar-bow circling the whole hemisphere. It strongly resembled the rainbow of the noon-day sun, only its colours were more soft, more mild, like the gentle tints of an Italian sky when sol's declining rays gild every object with his setting beams.

¶

10th day

The weather now has become very fine, with gentle breezes and a smooth sea. The nights are less dreary because we have a full moon. How beautiful is a moonlight night at sea! The vessel softly glides before the favouring gale whose gentle zephyrs waft her o'er the deep, while ten thousand little stars, reflected from a brilliant sky, sparkle beneath her sides, and all ocean smiles at the charming scene.

> The moon refulgent lamp of night,
> O'er heav'ns clear asure spreads her sacred light,
> When not a breath disturbs the deep serene,
> And not a cloud o'ercasts the solomn scene;
> Around her throne the vivid planets roll,
> And stars unnumber'd gild the glowing pole.

To enjoy such scenes as this Horatio would often steal away from the society of his noisy companions and feast his imagination with the memory of past joys. While pensively leaning over the vessel's side, marking her undulating motion, now mounting aloft upon the billows top and then sinking into the hollows depth profound. And listening to the watchman's mornful cry of "All's well," his soul would swell with

> many a proof of recollected Love.

There was a time when Horatio—the now wretched, forlorn, banished Horatio—lived in ease and affluence, enjoyed all the delights of society and possessed many an amiable friend who claimed a tender interest in his heart. Ye happy days of youthful enjoyment, alas! Where are ye now? Gone never to return. Yet perhaps Fate has still in reserve some future scenes of felicity to recompense a wounded heart for all its past sufferings and misfortunes. Perhaps, for who knows what hidden mysteries are contained in Fate's decree, the God of mercies may yet "temper the wind to the shorn lamb," and bestow a little angel upon Horatio, whose kindness and endearments will obliterate the remembrance of past misfortunes. If nature contains any panacea for the mind diseased, it must be the affection of a lovely woman.

O'er all the nerves what tender transports roll,
While Love with sweet enchantment melts the soul.

¶

14ᵗʰ day

Spoke the Portugese brig *Henriette*, Captain Jekins, from Madeira bound to Philadelphia. Captain Jekins informed us that the day before he was boarded by an officer from a British frigate. He said there was an American privateer cruising off Madeira, which had taken several prizes. The *Henriette* being short of bread, we supplied him with that necessary article and received in return some fruit. Wrote to her owner and permitted Cap. Jekins to proceed on his voyage.

Every afternoon when it was pleasant weather with a smooth sea the captain of marines exercised his men at the manuel exercise and taught them the several maneuvers necessary during an engagement. He found most of them acquainted with the use of the musket, tractable and full of activity and spirit. He has not the least doubt of their courage and fortitude in the day of battle and believes they will contribute as much towards a victory as the oldest seaman.

Often at the silent hour of midnight would Horatio retire from the heated cabin to taste the lucid coolness of the breeze, and seated upon a piece of artillery, which was intended to carry slaughter and destruction on board the enemy, indulge his melencholy fancy in feasting on the memory of departed joys. Then would imagination waft him to the dear soil of his native land, he would behold in idea his numerous relations and friends enjoying all the comforts and pleasures of domestic life; while he alas, was destined to traverse the treacherous ocean, subject to innumerable dangers, difficulties and perils. Horatio was formed for tenderness and love. Possessed of a warm and affectionate heart, endowed with great sensibility and alive to every softer emotion, he deeply felt the peculiar infelicity of his present situation and sighed for happier hours. Neither inclination, habit or education led Horatio to encounter the hardships and inconveniences of a sailor's life; but necessity and ill-health tore him from country, relations, friends, acquaintances, and all the sweet enjoyment of a literary life, to obtain health in foreign climates. Even seven long years of "wanderings around this world of care," and the thousand novelties presented to his view, could not banish the remembrance of former joys—joys now departed I fear never to return.

¶

16th day

This day was remarkably pleasant with gentle breezes and a clean unclouded horison. Our vessel rode proudly eminent on the floating tide. Every sail was spread to catch the favouring gale and waft her on her destined cruise. The officers had just assembled on deck from their convivial repast, when they beheld at a distance the whole ocean in a foam. At first they imagined it was a waterspout or whirlwind forming to windward, but they were soon convinced it was a more pleasing spectacle. Whales, porpoises, and dolphins, almost unnumerable, came sporting round our ship. The great leviathan of the deep moved in dreadful majesty through his watery kingdom, now rising to receive fresh animation from heaven's genial breezes and spouting a fearful catarack into the air, and then sinking beneath the boisterous surge, leaving a horrid chasm in his wake: sometimes approaching our stern and spreading his monstrous length far beyond the bows, and then diving beneath her keel, threatening us with instant destruction in case of coming in contact. Thousands of porpoises also,

> In circling wreathes now gambol on the tide
> Now bound aloft, now down the billows glide.
> Their tracks awhile the hoary waves retain
> That burn in sparkling trains along the main.

To make the scene still more delightful,

> A shoal of sporting dolphin they discern;
> From burnish'd scales they beam refulgent rays,
> Till all the glowing ocean seems to blase.

The officers instantly prepared their fishing apparatus and caught a great number of these beautiful fish. No object strikes the beholder with more pleasurable surprise than the appearance of the dolphin, both in the water and after it is caught. What renders this fish still more remarkable is, that it frequently changes its colour after it is taken til it dies, and always presenting to the eye the most brilliant appearance

> What radiant changes strike th'astonish'd sight!
> What glowing hues of mingled shade and light!
> Not equal beauties gild the lucid west,
> With parting beams all o'er profusely drest.
> Not lovelier colours paint the vernal dawn,
> When orient dews impearl th'enamel'd lawn;
> Than from his sides in bright suffusion flow,
> That now with gold imperial seem to glow;
> Now in pellucid sapphires meet the view,
> And emulate the soft celestial hue;
> Now beam a flaming crimson on the eye,
> And now assume the purple's deeper die.
> But here description clouds each shining ray;
> What terms of art can nature's powers display.

¶

18ᵗʰ day

We were all sitting at breakfast this morning, talking about the squally rain, thunder, lightning of the past night, when suddenly the officer on deck called out, *"A waterspout close aboard."* Instantly all of us ran upon deck, where we beheld the whole ocean in an uproar. Although a dead calm, the waves swelled tumultuously, the sky appeared inflamed, the sun was hid behind a dark cloud, and a vast column, resembling a huge pyramid, rapidly collected, extending itself into the clouds and embodying half of ocean's waves.

> The foaming base an angry whirlwind sweeps,
> Where curling billows rouse the fearful deeps.
> Still round and round the fluid vortex flies
> Scattering dun night and horror thro' the skies.
> The horrid apparition still draws nigh,
> And white with foam the whirling surges fly!
> The guns were prim'd; the vessel northward veers
> Till her black battery on the column bears.
> The nitre flies; and while the dreadful sound,
> Convulsive, shook the trembling air around,
> The watr'y volume, trembling to the sky,
> Burst down a dreadful deluge from on high!
> Th'affrighted surge, recoiling as it fell,
> *Rolling in hills disclos'd th'abyss of hell.*

¶

19ᵗʰ day

Spoke the Spanish brig *San Jose*, Captain Miguel Buigas, from Cadis bound to Santa Martha, with a cargo of wine, oil, fruits, olives, lady's veils, and musical instruments. Being tired of living on salt provision and desirous of a little novelty, we purchased of Captain Miguel some olives, preserved and pickled fruits, and two quarter-casks of wine, for which we gave him an order on our agent at Havana. This Spanish captain appeared to be a jovial pleasant old don, fond of good living and attached to the Americans. Having examined his papers, permitted him to proceed. We afterwards found his wine, fruits, and olives to be excellent.

Singular Ceremonies
on crossing the Line—*20ᵗʰ day*

Having crossed the Northern Tropic, the *Yankee's* crew prepared to perform the usual ceremonies on such an occasion. Accordingly, while the officers were at dinner, old Neptune, attended by his lady, his barbers and constables, dressed in the most fantastic manner, with black sheepskins round their bodies, their faces painted in diverse colours and large swabs upon their heads, serving both as hair and beards, with trumpets, pitchforks, shaving instruments etc., in their hands, hailed the *Yankee* and came on board. They were received with the discharge of cannon and three cheers by the whole crew. Neptune came aft and enquired of Captain Wilson whether he had any of his sons on board, and welcomed the famous privateer *Yankee* into his dominions. On being answered in the affirmative he asked permission to initiate the marines into the customary mysteries. Neptune then examined our surgeon and being convinced that he came to sea to take care of his children, he excused him from being shaved and passing through other disagreeable parts of the ceremony. After which Neptune and his comrades went forward and regularly initiated about one fourth of our crew into all the curious forms requisite to make them true sons of the ocean. The candidate for the character of a seaman was first blindfolded by the constables, then brought before the old sea-god and seated upon the side of the barge which was previously filled with dirty water, tar, slush, rotten onions, and potatoes, stinking codfish, bilge-water, and various other nauseous ingredients improper to mention: then Neptune with a loud trumpet asked him the following questions: "What is your name, age, occupation, and place of residence? What brought you to sea? What lady did you kiss first and what one last? Have you any wife or children, or do you expect to have any?" These questions he was bound to answer truly, being previously sworn on the seaman's bible, under the penalty of being chained to the pump or keel-hauled. During the time these questions were asked and the answers recorded, Neptune's lady frequently embraced her son, covering his face with red and black paint. After this the new seaman was sworn to these oaths, thus, "Never to leave the pump till it sucks, never to go up the lee-rigging in good weather, never to desert the ship til she sinks, never to eat brown bread when he could get white, unless he liked it better, never to kiss the maid when he could kiss the mistress, etc., etc." At the conclusion of every oath he was lathered by the barber with their new-fangled soap, composed of different coloured paint, slush, greese, dirt, bilge-water, gun-powder, & other delicious essences; the candidate was next shaved with an old iron-hoop, not quite so sharp as a razor and yet sharp enough to take off the beard, paint and sometimes a little of the skin. This being done he was ordered to hail old Neptune, the god of the seas, three times, and when he lifted the trumpet to his mouth one of the constables poured in a full discharge of *bilge-water*, which nearly suffocated the poor culprit. No sooner was this finished than Neptune and his companions seized the trembling frightened wretch and plunged with him into the deep, that is into the barge filled with the before-mentioned sweet ingredients. After washing him sufficiently in the briny tide, he was brought out and welcomed by Neptune and the whole crew as a true son of old ocean. The performance of these ceremonies occasioned infinite laughter and merriment. After the whole ceremony had concluded, the commander, officers, and whole ship's company joined in a ducking-match, which exited great good-humour and pleasantry. The remainder of the day and evening were devoted to fencing, boxing, wrestling, singing, dancing, drinking, laughing, and every species of mirth and fun.

I cannot say that I was altogether pleased with the above

ceremonies, as they certainly partook in some degree of cruelty and oppression. To say the least, it was sanctioning a barbarous custom, which has often produced fatal consequences. In the present instance, it materially injured the clothes of the marines, many of them were much bruised in the ducking scrape and the officers took violent colds from being wet when heated. The most amusing part of the scene to me was the terror and consternation of poor Cuffy Cockroach, our African prince: he came aft to the captain trembling and dreadfully alarmed: "Massa Capin, de debil is cum to kill de whiteman. He be one damn big black sheepman and hab one red and black face and too much hair on his head. He be stink too much and hab one great big knife. De Massa Capin dribe de debil away." When poor Cuffy saw the Devil shave and paint the marines, and the whole ship afterwards in an uproar, he seemed to think every body would be murdered and began to bellow and scream in the most frightening manner; but when the Ceremony was over and all again quiet, he said, "Eh! this buckra-man be de ver debil—he lov war-palaver too much—he be fight every day for noting—he be fight himself when he no see de Englishman and then he be dance and sing like de monkey—ha! ha! ha!"

¶

22ᵈ day

It is too true to be denied that there are moments when I feel a good deal homesick; when melancholy reflections will involuntarily rush upon the mind, filling it with regret and sorrow. Indeed it is extremely natural that a person who once pretended to a little education and refinement and has seen better days, when shut up in a small vessell, with no companions but a few rude, unpolished seamen, should occasionaly reflect upon the unfitness of his situation and wishes to be transported to different scenes. Why did Fate condemn me to be a wretched Wanderer? What dire offences have called down the perpetual vengeance of Heaven upon this unfortunate head? Alas! Conscience does not upbraid me with more than the common failings of humanity. 'Tis true I have erred, and who has not? True I have often felt the blush of contrition mantle my cheek for some involuntary error, committed in an unguarded moment, but still, as Heaven is my witness, never did I voluntarily sin against the laws of Virtue and Morality. And yet here I am, condemned to exile from country, relations, and all my dearest connections . . . 'Tis now seven long years since I was compelled by ill-health to abandon a lucrative and honorable profession, and all the sweet comforts of domestic life, to traverse foreign realms in search of that phantom Health, which continually flies before me. When just entered upon the career of life, Disease suddenly nipped the blossom of all my hopes: in one unhappy moment all my flattering ideas of Fame and Fortune took flight and left me nothing but misery and despair. I am now alas! a miserable outcast and wanderer:

Tis mine the vast and trackless deep to rove—
Alternate change of climate have I known,
I've felt the fierce extremes of either zone:
But while I measure o'er the painful race,
In Fortune's wild illimitable chase,
Adversity, companion of my way!
Still o'er her victim hangs with iron sway;
Bids new distresses every instant grow
Marking each change of place with change of woe.
Where'er I wander, thus vindictive fate
Pursues my weary steps with lasting hate.

¶

23^d day

A curious circumstance occurred this afternoon. While we were exercising our men at quarters, one of the prizemasters fired a pistol; shortly after a dolphin was caught and on opening it we discovered the identical ball which had been discharged as above-mentioned. This is certainly a very remarkable circumstance, and had I not personally witnessed it, should doubt its authenticity. If forcibly reminds me of a singular little story I read in some book, I forget what one. A lady, doubting the constancy of her lover, threw a favorite ring he had given her, with his name and this particular motto marked on it, "Lose me and you lose my Love," into the ocean, declaring she would never forgive him till he restored this ring. The lover shortly afterwards returned from a long absence, was immediately dismissed with the above declaration, without any explanation, and, in a fit of despair, again went to sea. It so happened, that he passed near the very latitude and longitude where this fatal ring had been thrown overboard . . . To amuse an idle moment and drive away the melancholy reflections which constantly haunted his mind, he diverted himself with fishing and caught a dolphin. When the sailor opened it for cooking, behold (singular to relate!) this famous ring was found unhurt and untarnished. The lover's satisfaction may easily be imagined, as well as the lady's surprise when he afterwards presented it and explained the manner in which it had been found. The story concluded with this excellent maxim, that the innocent ought never to despair, as every thing is possible to a just Deity.

¶

24th day

Having eat very heartily of the dolphin caught last night, we all become suddenly dull, sleepy, and much indisposed. The officers turned into their berths and slept in the most profound manner, in spite of every exertion to remain awake. I immediately suspected the cause of our indisposition, as I had often heard of the poisonous qualities of this fish and once severely felt the effects of it. Crossing the Bahama Bank our whole ship's crew were siezed with dizziness, incessant vomiting, loss of appetite, and almost total blindness from eating a dolphin. This is attributed to the fish's having fed on the copper banks and imbibed the pernicious qualities of that metal. Afterwards, during my residence at Nassau, the inhabitants showed me a variety of fish which were considered poisonous, in a greater or less degree, and some, particularly the rock-fish, that produced instant death. Those fish which possessed the most brilliant colours were always the most dangerous. To discover whether they were poisonous or not, it was customary to put a piece of silver (which attracts poison) into the cooking, which would become entirely black, or other wise continue unsoiled, according to the qualities of the fish. I personally witnessed the deadly nature of the rock-fish. Having visited Tusculum, the country seat of the Honorable Mr. Wyley, attorney general for the Bahamas, we caught one of these fish of a large size and brilliant colours. Not trusting to the usual experiment, a part of it was given to a dog and in less than twenty minutes after the animal eat it, he died in great agony.

¶

25th Day

Nothing on board the *Yankee* is so highly disgusting to me as the extreme indecency of language made use of by the cabin officers. Even profaneness, although both impolite and wicked, is less offensive than vulgarity in either words or actions. Swearing is so very common among seamen that even the most moral and religious become imperceptibly familiarized to it; but no man, who possesses the least delicacy or refinement can be pleased with blackguardism in action or discourse. I sincerely regret, that a man possessed of so excellent a heart and fine natural understanding as Captain Wilson, should be so fond of this kind of conversation. As to the other officers, little less could be expected, as neither their minds or morals rise above the common herd of mankind. I was pleased to observe, however, that on shore our commander threw aside entirely this worst part of a seaman's character and conversed with great propriety.

¶

27th day

At 11 A.M. Captain Wilson, while leaning over the starboard quarter, called out, "Land ho! right ahead." Instantly all hands ran upon deck and received the news with acclamations of joy. We knew it of course to be the Island of St. Anthony, one of the Cape de Verdes. Squared the yards, bore away, and ran down the whole length of the island within two miles distance. At the first sight the Island appeared mountainous, craggy, full of hummocks; and on approaching nearer we perceived it to be entirely steril, rocky, and uncultivated: not producing even a solitary tree to relieve the eye of the beholder from the dreary scene. It presented no appearance of being inhabited by man or beast. The mountains rose nearly perpendicular to the height of at least four thousand feet, forcibly reminding me of the Azores in that respect, but in no other, as the Cape de Verdes are only famous for being the most desolate and barren part of the world, while the Western Islands are celebrated as the supposed residence of the immortal Calypso.

These islands, twelve in number, are situated nearly due West from Goree, on the Coast of Africa, distant about 300 miles. Very few American vessels trade to these islands and indeed their commerce is of little importance.

Thus after being at sea twenty-seven days and crossing

the great Western Ocean, a distance of at least three thousand five hundred miles, we have safely arrived off the Cape de Verdes, the first of our cruising stations. Nothing very material occurred during our passage. At first we had a great deal of stormy dangerous weather, afterwards squalls, variable winds, calms, etc. We spoke only three vessels, caught only one fish, and had no opportunity to show either gallantry or courage.

We are now fast approaching the coast of Africa, the most sickly, pernicious climate on the globe. Our officers and company are at present in fine health and spirits, but how long they will continue to God only knows. Fevers, dysentarys, and various other fatal complaints, there attack the inhabitant of colder regions, and soon number him with the dead. Should we remain long on the station, probably many of our brave lads will sleep eternally on those sandy plains . . . And who knows but Horatio, the once happy Horatio, may be one among those unfortunates? Who knows but Fate has there condemned him to end his wretched days? Ah well! be it so—Misery and Horatio have been so long companions that he has become almost indifferent to future events. Misfortunes alone could have forced him to assume the profession he now follows, and to visit such countries as the savage coast of Africa. But

> He is one
> Whom the vile blows and buffets of the world
> Have so incens'd, that he would set
> His life on any chance to mend it,
> Or be rid on't.
>   —Macbeth

¶

28ᵗʰ day

While writing the subsequent account I am seated on the ruins of an old Portuguese fortification, erected on a high promontory in the Island of St. Nicholas. This fort is of very simple construction, being in the shape of a half-moon, with four embrasures; at present it is totally in ruins and has only two old four-pounders, one of which is dismounted and the other unfit for service . . . The view from where I now sit is peculiarly wild, romantic, and picturesque. Desolation broods over every surrounding object. Behind stupendous mountains lift their craggy heads above the clouds, which break around them; on each side are seen high broken cliffs and deep precipices; below a few miserable huts inhabited by coloured people, and in front the illimitable ocean, with our little gypsy dancing on the tide. Nature appears here to have sported in her wildest humour. Rocky, uneven, barren, not a sign of vegetation, for what purpose was this island created? On examination the rocks appear to be composed of lava and pumice stone, which raises a strong probability in the mind that this island and no doubt the rest of the Cape de Verdes, were thrown up from ocean's cave during some convulsion of nature.

At 4 o'clock this afternoon we landed on the rocks in a wide bay at the south end of this island. Five or six coloured men, between the Negro and mulatto, presented themselves on the shore and conducted us to three small huts built of stone without any furniture. We informed them we were in want of wood, water, and fresh provisions, on which they showed us a well situated in a most singular spot. We first entered a narrow footpath, which led winding under over-hanging precipices, then came to a gravelly beach, where we saw the masts, spars, anchors, guns, rigging, boats, and other materials belonging to a large armed ship; we en-quired concerning these things and found that an American had a short time since purchased a Portugese ship at Sierra Leone and passing this island in the rainy season, was ship-wrecked on this iron-bound shore and every soul perished. After passing this wreck, we walked through a kind of lane till we came to the well which was sunk to an amasing depth. On every side, except the one where we entered, the rocks rose to a fearful height, nearly in the form of regular columns, presenting one of the most wild and terrific pros-pects I ever beheld. Finding the water both brackish and sulphurious, we concluded it was not best to water here. We then enquired about the wood and fresh stock and found there was none of the former on the island and the latter was very dear and scarce, although we observed the mountains to be covered with goats. The blacks informed us there was a village two leagues distance in a fertile valley, which produced corn, grapes, oranges, and fruits of various kinds. Thinking it not advisable to remain any longer on this desert island, we purchased a few pigs of the natives, returned on board, and set sail for St. Iago.

¶

30ᵗʰ day

Running down the west side of the Isle of Mey with a fair wind and all sail set. This island has nothing very remarkable in its appearance. A long low point runs out a considerable extent to the southward, on which there is a small town, consisting of 20 or 30 tolerable looking houses and a great number of Negro huts. In front there is a sandy beach with numerous salt works upon it, and the background appears more green and fertile than that of the other islands we have seen. Having looked into the harbour to discover any English vessels and observing only two small Portuguese boats, we jibed ship and made all sail for St. Iago. Fine pleasant weather, a smooth sea, and all hands in good health.

¶

31ˢᵗ day
Arrival at St. Iago

At 1 P.M. we anchored in Port Praya, Island of St. Iago, having run from the Isle of Mey to this place, a distance of 9 leagues, in two hours. Captain Wilson, the surgeon, and purser went on shore in the barge. We were conducted by a black soldier first to the intendant, and afterwards by him to the governor-general. They received us in the most polite and friendly manner, and on being informed by Captain Wilson that he commanded the American armed brig *Yankee*, they expressed much surprise, and no little satisfaction at seeing us in this distant part of the world. When the commander asked permission to obtain a supply of wood, water, and fresh provisions, it was immediately granted. The governor, after enquiring about the events of the war between England and America, expressed much regret, as the war had entirely stopped the American trade to these islands. Formerly there were four regular traders to this port from different parts of America, who brought provisions and took salt in return. At present the island is entirely destitute of bread, rice, flour, etc., and the inhabitants make use of cassava, yams, and plantains in the room of these necessary articles. The governor said there had been lately no English vessels in the harbour but that the American privateer *Alfred*, Captain Williams, had touched in here a short time since for water and supplies. On taking our leave for the day the general said he should expect the customary salute, which should be returned.

The governor-general of the Cape de Verdes, Don Antonine Cotine del Ancastro, appears to be a man of about forty, rather stout, of a light complexion, and easy affable manners. He wore the English dress with the Order of the Holy Cross on his breast. His residence is decent enough for such a place as St. Iago, being built of stone, two stories, high and better furnished than Portuguese houses generally are. The floor however was abominably dirty, and I dare swear had not been washed these twenty years. His son and daughter were both in the room and appeared much fairer than the Creoles of the island. He was surrounded by soldiers and slaves.

The intendant, De Madina, and his residence bear a strong resemblance to the governor's, only he has this circumstance in his favor, that he speaks tolerable English, is a free-mason, and something of a merchant. He called on board the *Yankee* early on Wednesday morning, dressed in full uniform, with the general's compliments on our arrival, took breakfast with us, appeared pleased with our vessel and invited the officers to dine on shore with him and the governor.

St. Iago is undoubtedly the most important of the Cape de Verdes, both as respects size, population, and commerce. De Madina informs us, it is very fruitful beyond the mountains and produces everything in abundance; that it has several fine rivers, another considerable town called Ribera Grande, on the river of that name, and at least fifteen thousand inhabitants, mostly blacks. The white inhabitants are nearly all convicts . . . The harbour of Port Praya is spacious, of easy entrance, and perfectly safe, except when it blows a gale from the S.E. . . . The town, also called Praya, is situated on the top of a mountain and encloses an extensive plain, the houses forming nearly a circle. There are but four decent buildings in the town; one of these is a stone church, without a steeple . . . Both the port and town are well fortified, mounting about seventy pieces of cannon, extending in front of the town and on the mountains which surround it; most of which might be brought to bear upon a vessel entering the harbour. The place however is miserably garrisoned, being defended entirely by black troops without discipline, arms, or even decent clothing. Their cannon are rusty and many unfit for service; their muskets have no locks, at least very few of them; consequently the place could make but little resistance. I have not the least hesitation in saying that we might have surprised and taken the town without endangering a man; and had the Portuguese been enemies we no doubt should have tried the experiment. As they are friends we are much indebted to them for their civilities and attentions.

¶

33ᵈ day

According to invitation we all dined on shore with our new Portuguese friends. The Dinner was as good as the island could afford and cooked à la mode de Portuguese, that is, every dish was suffed with garlic and sweet oil.

During this day we finished getting off all our water, wood, live stock, and fruit, sufficient for a two months' supply. At 10 P.M. being a fine moonlight evening, with a fine fresh breeze, we took leave of their excellencies, Del Ancastro and De Madina, came on board, fired a farewell gun, got under way, and soon left Port Praya far behind.

Upon the whole we were all much pleased with the

friendly attentions of the Portuguese commanders, which, considering that Portugal is in strict alliance with our enemy, we had some reason to fear would not be the case. But it is a pleasing fact that both the Portuguese and Spanish subjects are more friendly towards Americans than towards their enemies, and were those governments independent of British control would no doubt manifest it in our favor.

¶

34*th* day

For several days past, I have been greatly indisposed with a variety of complaints, arising probably from change of climate, exposure to a burning sun, heavy dews, and perhaps in some degree from depression of spirits. I find indeed my feeble constitution incapable of bearing the thousand hardships and fatigues of a sea-faring life. Yet I will be contented to bear sickness and pain and misery, provided our cruise proves favorable to my interest; for it is my chief object at present to obtain property sufficient to discharge those little debts and obligations which long sickness obliged me to incur. Then I will strike a balance with the world, bestow the overplus, if any, upon my aged and beloved parents, and prepare to take my departure for the land of spirits. In truth I am almost tired with the wretched life of an invalid, and should resign my existence into the hands of its author with more pleasure than many

others would resign the meerest trifle. Indeed I begin to
think that

Life is the dream of a shadow.

¶

35th day

At meridian made Cape Verde, the westernmost part of
Africa. At the distance of five leagues the land appeared
like two large islands or rocks, suddenly rising in the ocean.
3 P.M. we passed within two leagues of Goree; the island
appears to be well fortified, having a large fort situated on
the top of a rock. We observed several fine large houses,
built of white stone, and a number of vessels at anchor
under the fort.

Night engagement

At 4 P.M. we discovered a schooner under full sail standing
out of Goree Harbour bound to windward. Made all sail in
chase. 8 P.M. finding we came up rapidly with the chase
and perceiving her to be an armed vessel, piped all hands to
quarters, and cleared for action. 9 P.M. showed a light in
the fore-rigging and fired several muskets as signals for the
sail to heave too—not obeying these signals, we fired a shot
under her stern—still continuing her course, we gave her
one of the bow guns double charged; upon which she im-

and should resign my existence into
the hands of its author with more
pleasure than many others would
resign the meerest trifle. Indeed I
begin to think that

"Life is the dream of a shadow"

35th Day.

At meridian made Cape
Verd, the westermost part of Africa.
at the distance of five leagues
the land appeared like two large
islands or rocks, suddenly rising in
the ocean. 3 p.m. we passed within
two leagues of Goree; the island
appears to be well fortified, having
a large fort situated on the top
of a rock. We observed several
fine large houses, built of white
stone, and a number of vessels
at anchor under the fort.

Page from the second journal showing the
34th and 35th days

mediately bore away and run down under our lee. As she
passed us our commander hailed her, "What schooner is
that?" Answer, "What Brig is that?" Captain again demanded, "What vessel is that?" Answer, "His Britannic
Majesty's schooner the *St. Iago.*" The British commander
then hailed us and was told we were "The United States
brig *Yankee*," upon hearing which he demanded, "How
we dared to fire into his Majesty's schooner!" and ordered
us to send our boat on board; our captain replied, "I shall
not—strike to me or I'll sink you." Instantly his Britannic
Majesty's schooner *St. Iago* wore short upon his heel and
luffed up close upon a wind, to prepare (as we supposed)
for action. Not thinking it advisable to engage at close-
quarters a king's vessel at night, without knowing her
force, we resolved to remain near her till morning, and
therefore stood after her under easy sail. 11 at night the
enemy gave us a shot which passed over us; we immediately
returned the compliment by giving him long Tom double-
charged with round and langrage. From that hour till 1 A.M.
the enemy continued firing, sometimes a single gun and
at other times a broadside, the shot either falling short or
passing over us; not one came on board, though frequently
within hail of each other. We determined not to be behind
hand with His Majesty's schooner and therefore gave him
gun for gun; whether we injured him or not it was impossible to discover from the darkness of the night. 2 A.M.
the commander thinking it still unadvisable to bring the
enemy to close action in the night, or to continue this kind
of warfare; and moreover believing that we should gain
nothing but hard blows and probably lose some of our men

or spars, without profit or advantage, even if we took her; ordered the master to make sail to the westward to deceive the enemy as to our cruising station. 3 A.M. lost sight of the enemy.

The officers and seamen remained at quarters upwards of *seven* hours and displayed great coolness and resolution. It was the general wish to lay the enemy alongside, but the commander's instructions were imperious, "never to engage a man of war when he could outsail them."

Although enfeebled by several days indisposition, the moment all hands were piped to quarters and orders given to clear for action, Horatio took his station as Captain of Marines, and discharged every necessary duty during the whole action—if such a trifling skirmish can be called so— the night dew was particularly heavy and Horatio felt its baneful effects. But, whenever Honor or duty calls, it is the province of a brave man to obey the summons.

> Life I hold but idle breath,
> When Fame or Honor's weigh'd with Death.
> —"Lady of the Lake"

For what is the value of Life without Honor, Fame, or Fortune? And how can a man better dispose of existence than in the cause of his country?

¶

41ˢᵗ day
Capture of the Mary Ann

At 6 A.M. discovered a sail bearing N.E. distant about three leagues. Set all sail in chase. Light airs, a smooth sea, and very pleasant. 7 A.M. made out the sail to be a sloop standing to the eastward, with her larboard tacks on board. 10 A.M. piped all hands to quarters, cleared for action, and fired a gun unshotted, upon which the sail bore down under our lee, with English colours flying at her main peak. Our commander hailed her and ordered her to strike her colours, which she did immediately. Sent our barge on board and found our prize to be the Sloop *Mary Ann* of London, Captain Stewart Sutherland, coppered mounting four carriage guns and navigated by nine persons, with a cargo of gold-dust, ivory, camwood, and palm-oil, bound home. Upon examination of the vessel and cargo, it was not deemed advisable to man her as a prize, but to take out the most valuable part of her cargo and burn her. Accordingly all our boats were employed in this business during the rest of the day. We received on board:

6 cannisters containing 452 oz. Gold-dust
500 elephants' teeth—one of them weighed 140 pounds
1 ton Camwood
156 muskets—4 cannon with apparatus

4 trunks Calcutta goods

Some bar-iron, palm-oil, gun-powder, beef, pork,
wine, goats, pigs, poultry, monkeys, parrots, etc.,
etc., besides her sails, spars, rigging, etc., etc.

The whole value received on board might be about $12,000.
Captain Sutherland estimated his vessel and cargo at $22,000.
She had been trading on the coast for some months and
was last from Dix Cove bound to Sierra Leone. Having
dismantled our prize, taken the prisoners and cargo on
board, we set her on fire and made sail on our course.

Captain Sutherland lives with the officers in the cabin
and the mate, his son, in the wardroom. Conscious that it
is a sufficient misfortune for our enemies to lose their property and to become prisoners of war, we feel it our duty to
render their sufferings as light as possible . . . We do not
war against individuals; we have no private revenge to
gratify; we know the peculiar hardships of the present war,
and we wish to soften its rigor as far as is consistent with
our commission. We are instructed to burn, sink, and
destroy, which compelled us to set fire to the *Mary Ann*.
But we never have, nor I trust we never shall, deprive an
unfortunate mariner of his private property or baggage.
The money, clothes, watches, and little peculims of every
prisoner we always restored to them. If we cannot acquire
wealth without robbing a poor prisoner of these necessary
comforts, we are contented to remain poor.

Captain Sutherland says that the whole of his little fortune, the remains of thirty years industry, is now in our
possession; he is not worth a shilling in the world. He tells
us he has a wife and seven small children in London and

God only know how they will be supported during his captivity and distress. This is not his first misfortune. Some years ago he lost a valuable vessel and cargo captured by a French privateer, who stripped him and his crew of every article they possessed in the world, and set them ashore naked and moneyless among the cannibals of Cape Palmas, yet he bears his troubles like a man and really, considering he is a Scotchman, possesses more philosophy than I expected.

¶

44th day

Captain Sutherland related to me a singular anecdote concerning the natives of Dix Cove. He says they worship the alligator and in particular one of a larger size than usual. They carry their idolatrous worship so far as daily to feed this ferocious animal. Being lately at Dix Cove he enquired of their king about the nature and truth of this worship and was convinced in the following manner. The king, according to custom, took a white fowl, went down to the borders of a lake, called several times in a loud voice, using certain mysterious words, when behold this hideous monster rose gradually out of the water, swam on the shore slowly approaches the sable monarch, received the customary offering, and again retired into his watry kingdom. This African god had thus been daily fed for upwards of

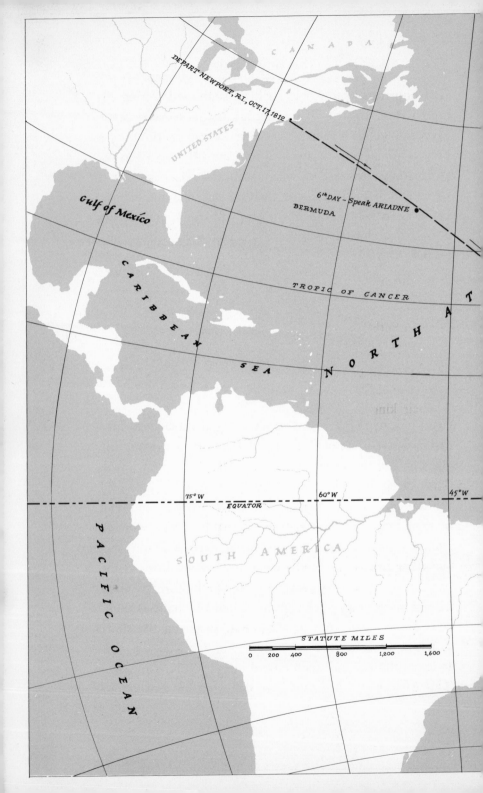

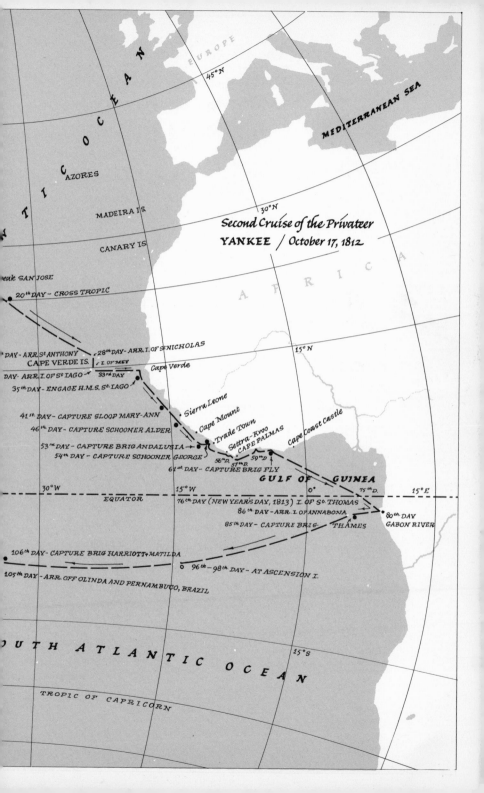

EUROPE

45°N

MEDITERRANEAN SEA

ATLANTIC OCEAN

AZORES

MADEIRA IS.

30°N

CANARY IS.

Second Cruise of the Privateer
YANKEE / *October 17, 1812*

AFRICA

reak SAN JOSE

20ᵗʰ DAY - CROSS TROPIC

15°N

DAY - ARR St ANTHONY / 28ᵗʰ DAY - ARR. I. OF S.NICHOLAS

CAPE VERDE IS. / I. OF MEY

DAY - ARR. I. OF St IAGO / 33ʳᵈ DAY

Cape Verde

35ᵗʰ DAY - ENGAGE H.M.S. St IAGO

Sierra Leone

41ˢᵗ DAY - CAPTURE SLOOP MARY-ANN

Cape Mount

46ᵗʰ DAY - CAPTURE SCHOONER ALDER

Trade Town

Settra-Kroo

Cape Coast Castle

53ʳᵈ DAY - CAPTURE BRIG ANDALUSIA

CAPE PALMAS

54ᵗʰ DAY - CAPTURE SCHOONER GEORGE

56ᵗʰ D. 57ᵗʰ D. 59ᵗʰ D.

61ˢᵗ DAY - CAPTURE BRIG FLY

GULF OF GUINEA

75ᵗʰ D.

15°E

30°W

15°W

0°

EQUATOR

76ᵗʰ DAY (NEW YEAR'S DAY, 1813) I. OF S. THOMAS

86ᵗʰ DAY - ARR. I. OF ANNABONA

80ᵗʰ DAY

GABON RIVER

85ᵗʰ DAY - CAPTURE BRIG THAMES

106ᵗʰ DAY - CAPTURE BRIG HARRIOTT+MATILDA

96ᵗʰ-98ᵗʰ DAY - AT ASCENSION I.

105ᵗʰ DAY - ARR. OFF OLINDA AND PERNAMBUCO, BRAZIL

OUTH ATLANTIC OCEAN

15°S

TROPIC OF CAPRICORN

forty years. Another singular circumstance is that this same aquatic deity always follows the king to his wars and neither fear or danger prevents his receiving his daily sacrifice.

¶

45th day

Among our black prisoners is a king's son, [who is] named Tom Wilson. He is upwards of six feet high, well proportioned, speaks a little English, is marked with a black streak from his forehead down to his chin to show that he is a Krooman and well disposed to all white men; he has no clothes on except a piece of blue basts to conceal those parts which even the most savage nations cover from the common eye. He wears a large string of glass beads of various shapes and colours round his neck, gold clasps round his wrists and ankles, and several little horns filled with unknown substances. These horns are called *fettish* and held sacred. Every time they drink the fettish has his share. All the nations of Africa believe in witchcraft and sorcery, and many of them offer human sacrifices to the devil to mitigate his anger. To what ridiculous follies and shameful cruelties will ignorance and superstition lead mankind? Happy is that man who possesses information and genius sufficient to penetrate these mysteries, avoid these follies, and rise superior to the common prejudices of his fellow creatures!

¶

46th day

For this week past the weather has been intensely hot. Indeed being within six degrees of the line we must expect to suffer from the heat. Unluckily it is almost constantly calm, with frequent thunder, lightening, and rain, which however does not cool the air. The nights are equally hot as the day, yet we dare not sleep on deck, as exposure to the heavy dews would be extremely dangerous. We are therefore forced into our small cabin, which is uncomfortable beyond all description. The excessive heat, the confined air, the mephytic smells combine to render it insufferable disgusting. I really apprehend a contagion, which will soon terminate our sufferings and our cruise.

¶

47th day
Dreadful explosion on
board the schooner Alder

At meridian continued in chase of the sail ahead; being nearly calm, with a smooth sea, got out the sweeps on both sides and the boats ahead to assist in towing the vessel.

Found we came up rapidly with the chase, which appeared to be a privateer built schooner, with a standing foreroyal and showing eight ports on a side. 2 P.M. fired a gun and hoisted English colours—not answered—we now supposed her to be the *St. Iago* and resolved to take her. ½ past 2 gave her another gun, upon which she hove too, hoisted English colours and prepared for action. 3 P.M. being distant about a mile and an half, hoisted the American flag and commenced firing our long twelve pounder. 4 P.M. got the boats astern, piped all hands to quarters and cleared for close action. Being now within half cannon shot, opened a brisk cannonade on the starboard side, which the enemy returned, her shot mostly passing over us or falling short, only one ball passing through the jib. At 20 m. past 4 P.M. the enemy observing that we intended to lay him aboard, filled away, made all sail, fired his stern. Chasers double-charged, and instantly blew up, occasioning a tremendous explosion. Observed the enemy's vessel to be on fire and saw several persons swimming along side. Immediately ceased firing, although her colours were still flying, and sent off our boats to save the lives of the enemy and extinguish the fire. The officers took up the swimmers, and then rowed alongside. The scene that now presented itself to their view was shocking beyond description. The vessel was still in flames, the quarter-deck was blown off, the captain was found near the mainmast, naked, mangled, and burnt in the most dreadful manner, one of the seamen lay near him bruised and burnt equally bad; a black man was found dead on the cabin floor and five others lay around him apparently dying. All these wounded men were carefully brought on board the *Yankee*, where they received every possible attention from the commander, surgeon, and other officers. Dr. Miller dressed their wounds, but found the captain and several black seamen in the most dangerous condition. The captain had two deep wounds in the head, which penetrated to the skull (probably from our langrage shot), his arms and legs were much bruised, his finger and toe nails all torn off, his hair and nearly all his skin burnt off, and his whole system greatly injured by the concussion. A small black boy presented a most singular yet distressing appearance. *He was literally blown out of his skin.* For some time after he was brought on board we thought he was white. The anguish and sufferings of these poor fellows must have been indescribably painful and excrutiating. Indeed I never beheld a more complicated scene of misery and distress. To see a number of fellow creatures thus burnt and mangled, to hear their piercing groans, and to reflect upon their perilous situation, just wavering on the brink of an awful eternity, would affect the most callous heart. What effect then must it have had on the susceptible feelings of an invalid? Sympathy also had her share in our commiseration. It forcibly occurred to every one that this fatal accident might have taken place on board our own vessel. Several times during the cruise, owing to the negligence of our gunner, we had been exposed to the same fate. On one occasion, whilst the commander was on shore at St. Iago, the gunner, being much intoxicated, entered the magazine with a lighted candle. At that moment hearing a noise I fortunately awoke from a partial slumber, seized the light or else we should all have been blown into eternity.

It was a lucky circumstance for the survivors of the *Alder's* crew that the magazine did not communicate with the hold, for there she had a cargo of four hundred casks of powder, and had that taken fire, it must have blown them and their vessel into ten thousand atoms. While our officers were extinguishing the flames and removing the goods, they were extremely terrified to find that the fire had approached with a few inches of this dreadful powderhouse. In fine, considering every circumstance, we have every reason to be thankful and for my own part, I never returned more heartfelt thanks that the night after this explosion, that it was not the *Yankee* instead of a British pirate, which the *Alder* proved afterwards to be. But to return to our prize.

Lieutenant Barton extinguished the flames and sent all the other prisoners on board the *Yankee*. Finding the prize no ways injured except in her cabin and quarter-deck, Lieutenant B. was ordered to remain on board during the night and to keep company with us.

On examination of the schooner's papers and log-book, which had escaped the flames, we found her to be a letter of marque called the *Alder* of Liverpool, formerly called *La Clarisse*, being a French lugger privateer, taken in 1809 by the *Cambrian* frigate. She was owned and commanded by Edward Crowley, mounted six nine-pounder (the rest of her guns were below), with a crew of twenty-one men. She left Sierra Leone nine days ago bound to the leeward on a trading voyage, with an assorted cargo of gunpowder, muskets, flints, bar-lead, iron, goods, beads, and sundries; she is a beautiful little vessel, sails fast, and is coppered to the bends. Vessel and cargo valued at $10,000.

At 2 A.M. Captain Crowley, notwithstanding every medical assistance, died in the greatest agony. For some hours previous to his disolution he appeared to suffer excruciating torments and when informed of his approaching end did not seem sensible of his situation. His body was committed to the waves with as much decency as was practicable. During the night the five black seamen died and were thrown overboard. The white seaman is just wavering between life and death; we fear he cannot recover.

The boatswain related to us the particulars which led to this horrid catastophre. He said the Captain stood at the helm, steering the vessel and giving his orders; that himself and several other seamen were stationed at the guns aft; that the stern chasers had no lashings and were double charged; that the instant one of them was discharged, it capsized with great violence, broke one of the quarter-deck planks and fell with all its fiery particles directly into the magazine, which was situated abaft the cabin and the vessel instantly blew up. The boatswain and another seaman, foreseing the danger, leaped into the sea the moment the gun was fired and thus saved themselves. It is supposed the captain was thrown into the air and fell into the main-rigging. The blacks whom we found dead were employed in filling cartridges in the magazine, and the others who were so dreadfully mangled were standing near the captain.

The *Alder* has several shot in her spars, sails, rigging, etc., and one 12 lb. ball stove her boat.

We were much surprised on overhauling the *Alder's* colours to find a *pirates* flag and pendant, which, one of his seamen informed us, his captain made use of in robbing the

Portuguese. This circumstance lessens our compassion for the fate of Captain Crowley, as it indicates a hostile disposition towards all mankind.

Hostes humane generis.

On a consultation of officers it was deemed advisable to repair our prize, man her, put on board the goods we had taken from the *Mary Ann*, send her to the Gabon, there to dispose of her cargo for gold-dust, ivory, gum, dye-wood, etc., and then set sail for America with the proceeds. Accordingly all this was accomplished, and our prize-master was instructed to assume the name of *Growley*, pass under the British papers and colours (we destroyed the pirates flag), trade with the natives as an Englishman, and pretend that his vessel had been injured by lightning. At 5 P.M. we took leave of our prize and set sail on our course, Cape St. Ann being in sight.

¶

49ᵗʰ day

At 12 midnight came on a most tremendous tornado. It blew, rained, thundered, and lightened in a truly terrific manner. Took in all sail and kept the vessel before the gale. The wind blew with a violence unequalled in northern latitudes, the rain fell in cataracts, the thunder seemed to

shake both heaven and earth, and the lightning rendered "darkness visible," to expose the horrors of the night. It struck several times close aboard and once the conductor saved us from destruction. Had the lightning penetrated the vessel's hold, she must instantly have blown up; the danger is very imminent on board an armed vessel both from the quantity of metal and powder on board. But the scene was terrific; every mind was filled with apprehension and alarm. No one who has not personally witnessed can imagine the congested terrors of a tornado.
For

> —Down at once
> Precipitant, descends a mingled mass
> of roaring winds, and flame, and rustling floods;
> In wild amasement fix'd the sailor stands,
> Art is too slow; by rapid fate oppress'd
> Our broad wing'd vessel sinks the briny tide.
>
> —THOMPSON

¶

50ᵗʰ day

Thus far I feel by no means pleased with our cruise. We have been at sea fifty days and have taken only two small prizes, which cannot divide more than forty dollars per share. Moreover there are several other circumstances which render this cruise less agreeable than the last. Our officers do not answer our expectations. Lieutenant Barton is to be sure a brave man and tries to act for the best, but he has not the faculty to command and therefore is little better than a common seaman. As to Lieutenant Vinson, he is a mere cypher; he is neither a sailor, a man of courage, and scarcely a man of common sense. During our late engagement with the pirate he appeared quite confounded, gave no orders about pointing the guns in his division, which was the first point of his duty, but stood like one of the pumps, senseless and immovable. Nay, even when the bulwarks took fire amidships, he had not the presence of mind to extinguish the flames, which exasperated Captain Wilson so highly that he reprimanded him severely and struck him with his trumpet. In fact the fellow is no more fit to command a division of guns, or take charge of a night watch than one of our powder-monkeys. The third lieutenant is both young and thoughtless. For these reasons and several others not necessary to mention, my present situation is extremely irksome. I would most willingly exchange it for the retirement of a lawyer's study. However here I am and here I must remain for at least four months longer.

Man never *is*, but always *to be* blest.

¶

51ˢᵗ day

It being Saturday night with pleasant weather, gentle breeze, a smooth sea, and the new moon just visible for the first time in the Western horizon, the officers and company drank a good health to all sweethearts and wives in some good old rum and Madeira, late the cabin stores of Captain Crowley. The marines than amused themselves with chanting psalms and hymns and made no contemptible music, the sailors in singing "Old Tom Tough and Old Tom Bowling" and the officers, in listening to the confused murmur as it rose upon the breeze of night.

At 9 A.M. Cape Mount bears right ahead distant about two leagues. Two canoes came off from the shore and the natives informed us there were no vessels at the cape of any description, nor had not been any for several moons. Accordingly, up helm, squared the yards and bore away for Mount Monserrada distant about forty miles to leeward.

Cape Mount, as the name indicates, is a mountain rising to a considerable height and covered with trees of various colours and descriptions, many of them in blossom. In fact this part of Africa is infinitely superior to any of the Cape de Verdes, which I can only remember as the most sterile part of God's creation. Between Cape Mount and Monserrada the land is low and covered with trees. Captain

Sutherland informs me the king of this country is called "Peter Careful" and is known to be a villain, robber, and cannibal. He makes no distinction between whites or blacks, but cheats, robs, and murders every person in his power, when it is his interest to so do . . . our black prisoners (26 in number) begged us for God's sake not to put them ashore among these Anthropophagi, as King Peter would certainly kill and eat them. Surely Hobbes' opinion is partially correct, that man in his natural state is always at enmity—against man.

¶

52ᵈ day

Monserrada is rather a high hill than a mountain. Several factories are established at this place and in good times carry on a brisk trade in slaves, ivory, wood, etc. The coast to the leeward of Monserrada is full of hummocks and covered with palm trees. It appears to be a low flat country with a sandy beach with a heavy surf breaking upon it. In some few places there are rocks at a short distance from the shore. But at the distance of a league from the shore you can run with perfect safety.

¶

53^d day
Battle with the Andalusia

The day commences with light airs, inclining to calm. Continued in chase of the sail ahead. At 1 P.M. made out the chase to be a large armed brig, showing ten ports on a side with English colours flying at her main peake and her main-topsail aback, apparently clearing for action. At ½ past 1 P.M. the enemy commenced the action, heaving every round shot over us and his grape falling short. Being at too great a distance for our carronades, resolved to stand on till we could close with the enemy without returning his fire, which would stop our headway . . . all sail set with light breezes: the enemy continued his cannonading; our men were ordered to lay down at their quarters; almost every shot now told—our sails and rigging were considerably injured. One nine-pound shot penetrated the bulwalks and went through the leeside, taking off the hat of one of the marines, without other injury. ½ past 2 P.M. the enemy filled away and made all sail standing in shore, keeping up a well-directed fire from his stern-chasers. ½ past 3 P.M. having approached, under a most galling fire, within good musket shot of the enemy, we gave three cheers and opened our whole battery upon him—giving him at the same time our starboard broadside and a volley of musketry—the enemy, not the least daunted, returned our fire and attempted to wave for the purpose of raking us—instantly luffed up and gave him our other broadside, the marines keeping up a continued fire from their muskets. The action now became warm and desperate. We possessed the advantage of sailing and therefore placed our ship on the enemy's larboard quarter, not deeming it yet advisable to board him. 20 m. past 4 P.M. observing that the enemy's fire became extremely faint and that his colours had been shot away in the early part of the engagement, our commander gave orders to cease firing. He then hailed her, asking if she had struck her colours and was answered, *"Not yet—don't be in a hurry."* We then recommenced firing with renewed animation, for about ten minutes, when having again silenced the enemy, we hailed him a second time with the enquiry, "Have you struck your colours." "Wait a moment and I'll tell you," was the answer. In a few minutes the enemy hailed us, "Are you *really* an American cruiser?" Answer, "I am." *"Then,"* replied he, *"I have struck to you upon the honor of a man."* Secured our guns and sent the barge on board. Found our prize to be the English letter of marque brig called the *Andalusia* of Gibraltar, Anthony Yates Kendall, master, 210 tons burthen, pierced for twenty and mounting ten carriage guns (six twelve-pound carronades and four long French nines) with small arms, ammunition etc., navigated by 100 men, including 80 free Africans, who assisted at the great guns or acted as marines. The *Andalusia* is owned at Gibraltar and was last from Sierra Leone bound to the Leeward, with an assorted cargo of Brandy, tobacco, iron, beads, dry goods, etc. It appears from her log that she lately captured the American brig

Three Friends and conveyed her into Sierra Leone, where the *Andalusia* sold all her wine porter, fine goods, etc., to the amount of $8,000.

The action between our little *Yankee* and the *Andalusia* lasted upwards of three hours, from the time the enemy fired his first shot till he struck. We engaged him forty-five minutes within pistol shot. Captain Kendall was wounded in the leg, the boatswain in the face, and one seaman in the shoulder, besides several blacks, the remainder of his crew owned their safety to his excellent bulwalks, which completely defended them against our grape and musket balls. On boarding the enemy we found her mainmast, foretopmast, and foreyard badly wounded; one twelve-pound shot in her hull, another entered the cabin and lodged in the captain's bed; nearly all her sails, braces, shrouds, running and standing rigging shot away, and every part of the vessel more or less injured. This effect we attribute to our langrage shot and iron-bars (about 3 feet long) which we discharged from our twelve-pounders. Three of the enemy's guns were dismounted and his deck covered with shot of different kinds.

The white prisoners were brought on board the *Yankee*. When Captain Kendall arrived on board he approached our commander, touched his hat and said, "This, sir, is a fortunate day for you, but a very unfortunate one for me; I have fought my vessel as long as possible, but hope you will not treat me the worse for it." Captain Wilson replied, "Certainly not; it is the fortune of war." Captain Kendall is a well-made handsome young man, genteel, and manly in his appearance, well informed, and every way quite the gentleman. Mr. O'Connor, the part owner and supercargo of our prize, is also a prisoner. He is, without exception, the most agreeable companion I have met with during our two cruises. Possessed of classical knowledge, a general acquaintance with belle-lettres, a particular fondness for the French, Spanish, and Italian languages; having traveled a great deal and made many judicious observations on men and manners, he is one of those well-bred Irishmen, whom we sometimes meet and who deserve our respect and esteem. Last summer Mr. O'Connor visited Fayal and is familiarly acquainted with Mr. Dabney's family. It gave me great pleasure to converse with this gentleman about a family whom I have every reason to love and esteem; and it gave me still greater pleasure to show some civilities to a person who is our prisoner and deserves both esteem and respect. Mr. O'Connor presented me with a small thermometer which I shall long keep in remembrance of a gentleman whom I should be pleased to meet hereafter under different circumstances.

Lieutenant Barton was ordered to remain on board the prize, with a strong watch to guard the black prisoners. At 6 P.M. we made sail in shore and came to anchor in 20 fathoms water. Trade town bearing N. E. distant about 2 leagues—our prize in company.

At daylight piped up all hands and sent part of the crew on board the *Andalusia* to repair damages, and to assist in landing the black prisoners upon their own native shore. The remainder of our officers and crew employed in mending our sails, splicing the rigging, cleaning the arms, and other necessary duty. On examining our vessel after the action found we had received considerable damage. One nine-pound shot in our hull, one grape in the mainmast, two shrouds and the weather fore brace cut away, and numerous shot through our mainsail, foresail, foretopsail, and jib—no person was killed or wounded. This is almost a miraculous circumstance, considering that we had ninety men at quarters, that our bulwalks consist only of a thin board, that the enemy defended his vessel with good courage and seamanship, and that the balls came rattling about our ears something thicker than hail stones . . . But Goodfortune still hovers o'er the *Yankee* and protects those brave lads.

> Whose march is on the mountain wave,
> Whose home is on the deep.

¶

54*th* day

Mr. O'Connor estimates his late vessel & cargo at twenty-nine thousand dollars, but I am confident they will not net us nine thousand dollars in America, as vessels are very cheap and her cargo is only calculated for an African market.

At 1 P.M. discovered a small schooner in shore standing to the northward. Weighe'd anchor and made all sail in chase. 2 P.M. it died away calm. Sent Master Snow with an

armed boat's crew to take possession of said vessel. At
4 P.M. Master Snow came to anchor under our lee with his
little prize and gave the following account of his adventure. He said that on approaching the chase he observed
her boat attempting to land on the beach, that he saw her
strike on a rock among the breakers, capsize, and the captain and crew swimming for the shore. That on going on
board he found her entirely deserted, as he expected, and
stripped of everything, except a quantity of rice stowed in
bulk. He immediately made sail and stood for the *Yankee*.
Our prisoners informed us that this schooner is called the
George, and is owned by Mr. Carr of Sierra Leone; that
she was formerly an American pilot-boat and was captured
with slaves on board about six months ago in the river
Gambia. She is about 60 tons burthen is a handsome little
vessel, but her bottom is very foul and her sails very poor.
As soon as she came to anchor, we sent all our boats to
take out the rice, and supplied our own vessel, as well as
the *Andalusia* with a sufficient quantity of this article. This
supply was very seasonable, as otherwise we would have
been compelled to buy it of the natives, for the purpose of
saving our bread . . . Captain Wilson did not consider the
George of sufficient value to send home and therefore, with
the hearty concurrence of his officers, made a present of
the vessel and remaining part of her cargo to Captain
Sutherland, late of the *Mary Ann*, as he had been the greatest sufferer by the capture of his vessel and moreover had
been fifteen days a prisoner on board the *Yankee*.

This morning a canoe came off from the shore with a
letter from Captain Goss, late master of the *George*. He

mentions that when he saw our barge approaching fear drove him ashore, as he thought we were Frenchmen; that when his boat upset, he lost all his ivory and goods; that when he got on shore, almost exhausted by swimming, those very natives with whom he had been trading the day before on the most friendly terms, robbed him of a small quantity of gold-dust he had secured about him and then stripped him of all his clothes. He prayed us most earnestly to take him on board, as his life was not safe among those cannibals. Captain Sutherland on reading this letter mentioned that he was well acquainted with Captain Goss and would take him on board the *George* bearing him to Sierra Leone.

At 11 A.M. having taken the paroles of all our white prisoners, giving them duplicates, we supplied them with every necessary article for their voyage, such as beef, pork, bread, rum, wine, a compass, and quadrant, etc., gave them all their baggage, clothes, private property, money, watches, etc. (Captain Sutherland had three watches, three hundred fifty dollars in silver, some gold bars, and several trunks of India goods.) We then sent them on board the *George*, and bid them farewell, and set sail in company with our other prize, standing down the coast.

Captains Sutherland and Kendall, Mr. O'Connor, and all the other prisoners expressed their thanks and gratitude for the kind treatment they had received while on board the *Yankee*. Indeed they could do no less; for the captains lived with the principal officers in the cabin, the mates in the wardroom, and the sailors in the fore-hold among our crew. Not one of them being put in irons, although our own safety demanded it, having 145 prisoners on board at this very time. In fact the President's Instructions enjoined it upon us to treat our prisoners with that humanity and kindness whichever ought to characterize a free and generous people.

¶

55th day

Thus having dismissed our white prisoners with the honors of war, and landed the Africans on their own shores, we prepared to send home our prize, the *Andalusia*. The purser made out a prize commission and instructions for Captain Wimpanny, gave all the brig's papers, sealed, with a letter to the owner, giving him a brief account of our cruise to the present day, and requesting him to congratulate our wise friends, the Federalists, on their sage prognostication, that the *Yankee* would be taken before she had been at sea 10 days. At 4 P.M., gave our prize three cheers, bade our comrades farewell, and set all sail standing down the coast.

¶

56th day

At 8 A.M. came to anchor off Settra-kroo, the principal town on the Grain Coast. Here the anchorage is perfectly safe, on a fine sandy bottom, about three miles from the shore, and one mile to the southward of several large black rocks, where the sea breaks with great violence. Settra-kroo is said to be the best and safest place to obtain water and supplies between Goree and Cape Palmas. The natives, being Kroomen, are very friendly, and the king's son, called Grand-loo (whom we took as a prisoner aboard the *Andalusia*), speaks good English, is an active intelligent fellow, well acquainted with the Americans, apparently honest, and upon the whole one of the best men you can procure for obtaining supplies or carrying on a trade with the natives. We had no sooner dropped anchor than his majesty Tom Nominee, king of Settra-kroo, came on board. He was greatly surprised to find his son a prisoner on board an American armed vessel, when he supposed him to be at Sierra Leone. They embraced and appeared highly affected with the meeting. The king is an old man, tall, and of a majestic appearance. He was very well dressed in loose robes made of bonnie blues, a handsome red mantle, a large quantity of coral beads, gold clasps, and rings, and a silver medal presented by a merchant of Liverpool, with various rich presents, for having retaken a very valuable ship and cargo from the crew, who had mutinied, killed the captain and principle officers, and run the ship ashore off Settra-kroo. His majesty's bodyguard were dressed in the robes of Paradise.

King Tom promised to fill all our water on condition of setting his son at liberty and giving up those articles which he had purchased at Sierra Leone as the result of several years' labor. This we agreed to and employed Grand-loo in exchanging a quantity of tobacco, powder, iron, etc., with the native for ivory, live stock, vegetables, fruits, etc. By this means we filled all our water and purchased a fine bullock, several sheep, goats, fowls, etc., also a large quantity of yams, plantains, bannanas, coco-nuts, oranges, palm-nuts, and wine (which I have heard much praised but think very insipid, as it tastes like honey, vinegar, and milk), pine-apples, sugar-cane, porcupine quills, etc.—all these things we procured very cheap for a little damaged tobacco, gun powder, etc. At the present moment there are at least one hundred canoes alongside, containing perhaps four or five hundred native africans, most of them in the dress of nature. Their language seems like a medley of confused sounds and composed of few words; their gesticulation is continual and expressive; their screaming and chattering similar to the monkeys and parrots, which they bring off for sale. Indeed few of them possess a superiority of intelligence to these animals. Both the king and prince of Settra-kroo were anxious to sell us a few hundred slaves, informing us they had lately taken a great many prisoners from the neighbouring town, and unless they sold them, must put them to death. This not being our present business, we took leave of his black majesty and our Negro friend,

Grand-loo, making them several presents, weighed anchor, and made all sail bound to leeward.

Longitude 7° 48′ W.—Thermometer 106° in the sun

¶

57ᵗʰ day

At 5 P.M. hove to off the town of Grand Sisters, thirty miles to windward of Cape Palmas, about two miles from the shore. Sent in our barge to land Tom Wilson, son to the king of Grand Sisters, whom we took prisoner in the *Mary Ann*. This prince, as well as Grand Loo, had been of great assistance to us in procuring water, fresh stock, etc., and in trading with the natives as we sailed down the coast. He not only speaks a great many of the African languages, but also good English and is an honest, good-hearted fellow. Captain Sutherland recommended him in the highest terms. When our barge landed we observed a vast collection of Tom Wilson's countrymen drawn up on the beach in battle array . . . This was owing to their being at war with their neighbours, the natives of Little Sisters. They were even apprehensive of coming off to our vessel, for fear their enemies should intercept their return. Tom Wilson said he should now be a great warrior, for white men had learned him war palaver and given him a musket, some powder and balls. Grand Sisters is a large town, containing a great number of thatched huts, situated in the midst of palm groves, plantain walks, and rice fields, presenting a most pleasing and picturesque appearance.

10 A.M. passed the famous Cape Palmas, distant about three leagues. It has no distinguishing mark, except a small rise in the land and numerous lofty palm trees.

Latitude 40° 26′ N.

¶

58th day

Killed our bullock and had a most sumptuous feast. The African cattle are not one-third the size of the American ox, they have very short legs, no horns, and smooth black hair. The sheep and goats are also much smaller than in colder climates, and it is something singular that the former have no wool but long coarse hair, without horns and much resemble goats. The flesh of the bullock is red, very lean, but tolerably tender. We have an abundant supply of fish, particularly a large kind of flying-fish, which are most excellent.

¶

59th day

As you approach the bay of St. Andrews, the land rises to
a considerable height, and is covered with lofty trees to the
very summit. There is no appearance of cultivation . . .
This afternoon fresh breezes cool and extremely pleasant;
running down the Gold Coast with great velocity in hopes
of capturing several vessels which we understand are trading at Cape Lahou.

8 A.M. a canoe came off from Piccininny Cape Lahou
and the natives informed us of a brig, mounting six guns,
which sailed a few days before for Cape Corde Castle. The
natives of Grand and Piccininny Lahou are at war with
each other, and the former burnt the town of the latter
night before last. They brought off gold-dust and ivory
which they exchanged for powder and muskets.

¶

60th day

Antonio, king of Grand Cape Lahou, came on board in
a war canoe, attended by fourteen of his nobility. His sable
majesty confirmed the news we received yesterday rela-

tive to the English brig. These natives are something blacker than ebony, very stout, well proportioned, of a warlike ferocious aspect, with their hair and beards platted in the most fantastic manner. After King Antonio and his nobility had got as drunk as David's son, we were obliged to force them out of our vessel.

At 7 P.M. came on a tremendous tornado, attended as usual, with wind, rain, thunder, and lightning. The whole hemisphere seemed to be on fire. The thunder appeared to shake the ocean to the center and the wind blew with unheard-of violence. One stroke of lightning again struck our conductor and nearly blinded every person on deck, but did no injury to the vessel.

> In a huge deluge bursts the living flame,
> And dread concussion rends the etherial frame.

¶

Capture of the brig Fly
under the guns of Fort Apollonia

At 10 A.M. discovered the brig before mentioned under the guns of Fort Apollonia at anchor. 1 P.M. piped for volunteers to man the barge and cut her out. Several officers and nearly the whole crew came aft and offered their services. The commander requested Lieutenant Barton to head the expedition and to select his men. Upon which he chose twenty-one of the most able and experienced seamen who were properly armed for the purpose. 4 P.M. piped to quarters and cleared for action. It was understood that the *Yankee* should run in under *English* colours until she came within half cannon shot of the enemy, then send off the barge with the lieutenants, another officer and six bargemen, dressed like Englishmen, only visible, the rest being concealed under the boats' sail. In case the barge should not be able to carry her, or the fort should open upon them, then the *Yankee* should instantly lay her alongside, and return the fire from the fort.

According to this plan at 4 P.M. we rounded to within musket shot of the enemy and sent off the barge. Every heart beat high with anxiety as they saw her approach the enemy. In six minutes they were alongside and took possession of the prize. Not a shot was fired. Lieutenant Barton instantly cut the cable, made sail, and stood out to sea close on a wind. The *Yankee* now filled away and fired two twelve-pound shot directly into the fort, which (strange to tell!) were not returned.

Lieutenant Barton mentions, that when he got alongside of the enemy, and all hands completely armed jumped on board, the captain came forward and surrendered himself and vessel, but the mate ran into the cabin, seized a pistol, and was in the act of firing at one of the master's mates, when he struck it out of his hand.

We find our prize to be the English copper bottomed brig *Fly* of London, Johnathan Tyderman, master, 100 tons burthen, mounting six nine pounders with small arms, ammunition, etc., and navigated by eleven men, besides blacks. The *Fly* was formerly a French privateer, built at the Isle of France, is a new and very handsome vessel, sails remarkably well, and has a valuable cargo of gold-dust, ivory, gunpowder, and dry goods. The *Fly* captured on the 29th instant the Portuguese sloop *New Constitution* (supposed to be American property) with 81 slaves on board and sent her to Sierra Leone for trial.

Captain Tyderman states, that altho the Castle of Apollomia mounts 50 pieces of heavy artillery, yet it has but a small garrison, and the commander at this time is gone down to Cape Coise Castle to pass the Christmas holidays. He says we might easily land and take possession of the fort, but it would not pay us for our trouble. Captain Tyderman further mentions that he supposed us to be an English man of war, made no preparations for defending his vessel, but was actually weighing gold-dust at the time our officer surprised him. Had he suspected our real character he would have run his vessel on shore, landed his gold in the castle and there defended it.

Took the paroles of the white prisoners and being within sight of Apollonia, at the request of Captain Tyderman gave him his long-boat and permitted him and his crew to go on shore, restoring all their clothes, baggage, money, etc., besides several presents. Yet to say the truth, this captain little [deserved] such treatment, for of all the monsters which a seafaring life engenders, the captain of the *Fly* is the most brutal. Ignorant yet presumptuous, assuming, without merit, prejudiced, passionate, cowardly, his person corresponding to his mind, large, rawboned, harsh features, dark complexion, and speaking with the uncouth accent of a real cockney. This is a true picture of that ferocious brute Tyderman. He disgusted every officer on board the *Yankee* by his boasting swaggering conduct. He even had the daring presumption to introduce his black mistress into our cabin. No one except Captain Wilson, whose forbearance is truly astonishing, could have overlooked so gross a violation of decorum. In fact I never met with a person whose appearance, manners, and language created such sovereign disgust and hatred.

The following articles were taken out of the *Fly*, namely:

800 ounces gold-dust and bars

4 ton of Ivory

20 casks of gun-powder

a quantity of shot

6 dozen ducks

3 sheep

4 dozen fowls

100 yams

5 goats

Rum, brandy, porter, Madeira, and port wine, all of the best quality, pickles, anchovies, and a thousand other valuable little articles. This supply was quite seasonable and you may be assured we had a jubilee. Among our prisoners on this occasion we have the pleasure to mention about 200 monkeys and parrots! Query, will they answer in exchange for our Canadian heroes, the Hulls, Rensalears, and Winchesters of America?

Appointed Ths. Milton prize-master of the *Fly*, wrote a letter to the owner, and at 11 A.M. bade him adieu.

¶

65th day

The commander resolved to leave the coast of Africa immediately as we have information of the *Kangaroo* sloop of war being a few leagues to leeward and the *Amelia* frigate in pursuit of us to windward. Having occasioned no little disturbance between Goree and Cape Apollonica, having looked into every port between these places, except Sierra Leone, and taken every vessel we have heard of, it would neither be safe or politic to remain longer on this station. We shall now stand off to sea, and run for the Island of St. Thomas, for the purpose of filling our water and obtaining supplies.

¶

69th day
Christmas Day

At sea, off the coast of Africa, pleasant gales, a smooth sea, and remarkably pleasant weather.

Little did Horatio imagine last Christmas, when he was a resident on the Dee-side, in Jamaica, that one little twelve months would have metamorphosed him into an officer on board of an American privateer, and transferred him to the burning clime of Africa. 'Tis curious to consider how a few months may change the situation of man. For these seven years past scarcely has Horatio remained a month in one place. Continually traveling by land or water, in hopes to conquer the fatal disease that preys upon his constitution, or at least to find some alleviation in the novel and various scenes of foreign countries. Although disappointment always met him on the distant shore, yet hope flattered him to persevere.

When I fairly estimate the happy and unhappy days of the past year, I find the former so few and the latter so numerous, that my heart sinks at the sad reality, and hope almost expires under the load of human miseries. The first four months of the past year, I was an exile among strangers in Cuba and Jamaica. There I found little enjoyment. The dissipated lives, the luxurious banquets, the midnight carousals of these Indian Nabobs were little congenial to the habits or feelings of an invalid. I returned to Charleston and there suffered the severest pangs of sickness. I fled to Providence, there my health improved, and I became tolerably contented, when necessity induced me to enter on board the *Yankee*. Was I happy during my first cruise? By no means. Yet there were some few days which passed off in hilarity and mirth. The cruise upon the whole was not disagreable, and I wish the present one might prove equally so. We returned victorious and successful. This was gratifying. I mixed again in female society. The contrast from storms and hurricanes, war, and bloodshed, terrors and dangers, to all the pleasures of domestic life, the fascinating smiles of lovely woman and the thousand charms which society present, gave a double zest to every enjoyment. This was happiness. Prudence took flight and Indulgence stood at the helm. Every sail was spread to catch the gentle breezes of Friendship and Love, which wafted me on the smooth ocean of delight into the harbour of Enjoyment. In fact for one little month I was happy, at least as nearly so as a man of pleasure can be. But the time approached when I was again to leave this fairy scene of happiness, to traverse old Neptune's boisterous domain. Gloom and disappointment seized upon my mind, and unpleasant forebodings told me I should never return alive. Happiness was at an end. I again bade adieu to country, relations, friends, and all the dear connections of life and entered on this long and dangerous cruise. What will be the issue God only knows.

The thermometer now stands at 90° in the cabin; the weather is of course excessively hot; being nearly under a vertical sun its rays are insupportable. At night we can scarcely breathe in the cabin from the heat and confined air, combined with the mephytiegass [sic] (as our surgeon calls it)—during the day we have an awning over the vessel which renders us more comfortable.

Latitude 1° 46′ N. — Longitude 3° E.

¶

72ᵈ day

Spoke the little Portuguese schooner or boat (14 tons burthen) called the *Antonia de Santa Rosa de Lima*, Captain Felix, 5 days out from St. Thomas's bound to Prince's Island with 27 slaves on board and manned by 9 black seamen. This black navigator had lost himself and was steering N.W. instead of E. by S., which was his true course. No doubt this boat had in reality brought off these slaves for some Portuguese vessel for the captain was greatly alarmed when we hoisted English colours.

¶

75ᵗʰ day
Arrival at St. Thomas's

As you approach the Island of St. Thomas from the westward, the land gradually rises from the northern and southern extremities, till it forms a high mountain in the centre, covered with clouds. At the north end you observe a great number of green fields with numerous coco-nut and plantain groves.

At 6 P.M. came to anchor in man of war bay, about two miles from a low sandy beach, the background covered with vegitation.

This morning the commander and purser went on shore, waited upon the governor and Fiscall [judge], were received with attention and politeness, obtained permission to fill our water and were promised a supply of livestock, vegetables, fruit, and other necessary articles. They were invited to dine on shore but Captain Wilson declined the invitation wishing to return on board to expedite the watering.

The governor said he had no official notice of the war between America and England. In fact a British ship touched at the island eight days ago who assured him all differences between the two governments had been amicably settled. He informed us of several English merchantmen trading in the river Gabon, particularly a large letter of marque ship mounting eighteen 12v's with 45 men. He expects the *Amelia* frigate daily at the island on her way to Brazil. It appears that most of the British men of war touch here and at Prince's for water and supplies.

The governor and fiscall [judge] spoke in high terms of the American government and people, were pleased to hear that [Portugal] and America were still on friendly terms, and expressed the highest indignation against British Pride and Insolence. They mentioned that the British cruisers capture all the Portuguese vessels on the coast, nay that they had taken several out of Brazil, under various frivolous pretences, and in consequence thereof the mob had stoned the English consul to death.

¶

76ᵗʰ day
Friday, New Year's Day, 1813

We filled all our water in about six hours at a fine, clear
rapid river, about one hundred yards from a white house
on the beach, opposite to where we anchored. We also cut
as much wood as was necessary and obtained a large supply
of coco-nuts merely by cutting down the trees. This fruit
when nearly ripe is peculiarly delicious. The nut is filled
with a kind of milk both cooling and extremely nutritious.

> Oh, stretch'd amid there orchards of the sun,
> Give me to drain the Cocoa's milky bowl . . .

In the afternoon an officer came on board with the governor's compliments, and mentioned that he would supply
us with every article we were in want of and send them
down in canoes, without obliging us to beat up the city.
Sent a note expressive of our thanks on the occasion.

This morning the commander and purser again visted
his excellency, Don Juan Ferreira Guimaraens, the gov-
erner, and Don Raymond Jose da Cuinba Matos, the fiscall
or judge, and were received as yesterday with great civility
and politeness.

It being New Year's Day and a great festival we attended church. It is a small inelegant building and what
appeared very singular to us was, that all the priests, monks,
females, and whole congregation were mulattoes and blacks.

They chanted most enchantingly through their noses, and repeated the Te Deum's and Gloria Patre's in the true Creole and Africain lingo. The oderiferous effluvia from these sable penitents was too exquisite for our olfactory nerves, therefore we strolled through the city and returned to the governors.

From his balcony we saw a procession, civil and military, composed of the principal inhabitants of the place (all coloured people), with two bands of music, not quite so bewitchingly harmonious as an Italian orchestra, and the Virgin Mary, parading the streets.

We dined at the governor's and had a most superb dinner composed of ten different dishes, cooked in the Portugese style, with all kinds of vegetables, such as green corn, cucumbers, melons, etc., fruits, sweetmeats, liqueurs, wine, porter, coffee, etc., etc. Eleven slaves attended at table, while several others played on different instruments of music in the adjoining room. We remained on shore the rest of the day, as it came on to rain very heavy. The governor having sent on board every article we wished to procure, we paid him the amount in gold-dust. We then bade him and the fiscall [judge] adieu, thanked them for all their civilities, returned on board and at 11 P.M., weighed anchor, and stood out to sea with a fair wind.

St. Thomas's is a beautiful fertile island, forty-five leagues in circumference, producing coffee in great abundance and of a superior quality; also corn, spices, vegetables, and tropical fruits of every description; cattle, sheep, goats, hogs, turtles, fish, etc.

The town is situated at the head of a fine bay, in the

shape of a circle or half-moon and contains perhaps three or four hundred houses, interspersed among flower gardens, plantain groves, and coffee-walks. Most of the buildings are mere huts, the convents and many of the largest houses in ruins and the remainder by no means elegant. The fort or castle on the left hand as you enter the port, mounts forty pieces of artillery with a garrison of one hundred men.

This island situated on the equator and $7°$ E. Longitude, is said to be the most sickly place in the world. The heat is excessive and quite insupportable. It rains during the whole of our summer months, but the present season is their summer and the most sickly part of the year, from the intense heat of an unclouded sun . . . This is the first of January and yet the thermometer stands at 94 degrees in the cabin and nearly boils in the sun. No doubt our friends in America are freezing under their snowbanks and icicles and shivering before the Northern blast, while we, almost five thousand miles distant, are gasping for breath in the torrid zone and under the sun's perpendicular rays. We however have one advantage. We are feasting on green corn, cucumbers, melons, and all the delicious fruits of a summer climate, while they are half-starving on their fat geese and turkeys, their carrots and parsnips and other long sass.

I purchased six beautiful little parakeets, in a beautiful cage, for my beautiful little friend at Bristol. Also a marmoset, resembling a Franciscan friar, for my young nephews. The birds in this climate have the most brilliant plumage but do not excel in singing.

¶

78ᵗʰ day

Latitude 6 miles South—Thus we have passed the equator or Grand Divisional line of the globe. We omitted the ceremonies usual on such occasions, having already performed them once and the excessive heat of the weather might produce fevers and perhaps death. I feel a kind of joy and satisfaction in having passed the center of the earth, an event that does not happen to one out of a thousand.

We are now bound to the Gabon in search of the letter of marque before mentioned.

¶

80ᵗʰ day

At 7 P.M. came to anchor at the mouth of Gabon river, in 10 fathoms water—a remarkable tree is visible on sandy point, but the land is low on each side of the river. Immediately piped for Volunteers to man the Barge and explore the river in search of the enemy. Master Snow was appointed to command the expedition and twenty-two brave fellows selected to accompany him. They were all completely armed and supplied with every necessary article for their night campaign. At 20 min. past 7 P.M. the Barge left the *Yankee*, with the best wishes of their remaining companions for their success and safe return.

During the night it was calm and intolerably hot, the thermometer standing at 90° at midnight.

At 9 A.M. we discovered two large boats in shore standing towards us full of men. Piped all hands to quarters, cleared for action and got a spring upon the cable. Shortly after two African kings came on board, who informed us, there was a Portuguese schooner trading for slaves high up the river and that an English cutter arrived three days ago at King Glass's Town. From their description of this last vessel, her captain, and cargo, we were clearly convinced that this cutter was no other than our prize the *Alder*. Captain Salisberry, our prize-master, when he arrived passed as an Englishman told the natives he had been fired into by a Portuguese ship at Rio Pungus, that one shot stove his boat, that he had been struck with lightning during a tornado, which blew up his quarter-deck and killed the former captain and five seamen. Under this description he passed as an English vessel. These natives further informed us that the two brigs we heard of at St. Thomas's sailed with valuable cargoes two weeks ago, and that the ship had not arrived.

At meridian the barge returned on board and Master Snow informed us, that they had proceeded up the river about twelve leagues, that they saw no English vessels, but heard of the Portuguese schooner; that on their return they boarded the cutter above mentioned, and found her really to be our prize the *Alder*. Captain Salisberry said he arrived in the river five days ago, that he was making a rapid and profitable trade for ivory, beeswax, dye, woods, and gold-dust, that he expected to sail for Bristol in about a week and that his crew were in good health.

¶

81st day

At meridian weighed anchor and stood out of Gabon river bound to Annabona for supplies.

¶

85th day

At daylight saw Annabona ahead distant about three leagues, and a large Brig standing in for the land. Made all sail in chase, upon which the brig hove to, hoisted English colours, and showed seven ports on a side. Piped all hands to quarters and cleared for action. At 7 A.M. ran down alongside of the enemy and ordered him to strike his colours, which he did immediately. Sent the barge on board and found her to be the English brig *Thames*, Francis Toole, master, 171 tons burthen, mounting eight twelve-pound carronades, with small arms, ammunition, etc., from May-jumba, Africa, bound to London, navigated by fourteen persons, with a full cargo of camwood, ivory, and goods. Took the prisoners on board and sent Mr. Geo. Eddy as prize-master of the *Thames*. This vessel is coppered, thoroughly repaired and carries a large cargo. Estimated at $30,000.

¶

86ᵗʰ day
Arrival at Annabona

At 5 P.M. came to anchor on the north side of the Island of Annabona, opposite a small village, about a mile from the shore. Soon after we anchored, the black king and his prime minister came on board. He was an old ugly Negro, had a piece of coarse red base wrapped around him as a mantle, no shirt, an old worn-out pair of nankeen breeches, a thread-bare pair of stockings with numerous holes through which you saw his black skin, a pair of shoes cut out of boots, and an ancient strumpet's cap put wrong end foremost on his curly head. We easily obtained permission from this most notable monarch to wood and water. At daylight this morning employed all hands in filling our empty water casks, getting off wood and purchasing livestock, vegetables, and fruits, from the natives. Having finished our trade and filled our water, at 11 A.M. set sail bound to Ascension and from thence to the coast of Brazil.

The Island of Annabona is seven or eight leagues in circumference, and is composed of one continued mountain, covered with orange, lime, and coco-nut trees, and green herbage to the very summit. It has a fertile and beautiful appearance.

'Tis with much regret I mention the loss of all my little parakeets. The cage was broken either by accident or intentionally, and all these little birds took their flight from their prison.

¶

90ᵗʰ day

We have now been at sea three months, one-half of our cruise. It is a long time to be confined on board a small vessel and appears to me ten times longer than it really is. There are a thousand disagreeable circumstances attending a sea-faring life. Among the worst are the companions whom we are obliged to associate with. Sailors, though candid and generous, brave and honest, are generally rough and unaccommodating, arbitrary, and passionate, careless of pleasing or giving offence. Their conversation always turns upon their own adventures, or else dwells upon the disgusting pleasures of the Bagnio. My own heart tells me that the nice sense of Honor, of Virtue and Religion which education and habit formerly planted there, is now almost lost amidst the corrupt morals, and indecent conversation of the sea-monsters. The ease and politeness which give so many charms to society, are found unnecessary, nay, ridiculous among these unpolished sons of Neptune; these were consequently laid aside, and succeeded by vulgarity of behavior and discourse. I really much fear that both my manners and morals have been greatly injured by associating with these *Yankee* tars. Whether a return to society will reestablish those virtues of the head and heart, without which man is a brute, is something doubtful. Habits are powerful and inveterate. However reason and good sense will work miracles, and I am firmly resolved to eradicate from my mind all those baneful impressions, which war, bloodshed, and murder have implanted there.

¶

96*th* day
Arrival at Ascension

At 5 P.M. came to anchor off Ascension Island, about half a mile from the shore. Sent the barge on shore for the purpose of procuring turtle during the night. In the morning it returned with two fine large green turtle, weighing upwards of four hundred pounds each. The purser then wrote a letter mentioning the arrival of the *Yankee* at the island, her successful cruise, and the declaration of war against

England, which letter he directs to any American captain
who might hereafter touch at the island. The intention of
writing this letter was to give notice to our homeward
bound India men of the war, that they might avoid its consequences. It was enclosed in a bottle, sent on shore and
deposited in the post office, as it is called, that is among the
rocks, where we observed a number of names engraved,
particularly the following, "Young, Dickenson 1813,"
"Crescent, Leach, Salem 1812."

We caught a great number of fish and killed many
birds, neither fit to eat.

The Island of Ascension is three leagues in length and
two in breadth. It is composed of several hills or hummocks,
covered with a reddish earth, and has a very rocky craggy
and rugged appearance. It was evidently thrown up by
some convulsion of the earth; it looks like

> the fragments of an earlier world.
> —WALTER SCOTT

It is not inhabited and produces neither tree, vegetable,
fruit, grass, nor even fresh water, except in the rainy season.
We discovered a few wild goats on the mountains and
rocks, a vast number of ship rats in the valleys and almost
innumberable sea birds, which were so tame that our officers
killed them with stones and clubs and with difficulty kept
them from lighting on their heads. This island is principally
resorted to, by vessels bound from Africa and the East
Indies, to procure turtle, which are found here in great
abundance from November to March. These turtles are
easily taken. The sailors go on shore in the night, conceal

themselves near the beach, and when they observe the turtle ascending the beach to deposit their eggs, rush upon them, capsize them upon their backs and carry off their prizes in triumph next morning. The turtle caught here are said to be of the finest and most delicate flavour. It is really wonderful to consider the quantity of eggs they contain. On opening our largest turtle we took out of him three large buckets full, in number, 7,000.

¶

97th day

The officers and company feasted most luxuriously on the turtle they caught last night. We had soup, and stakes, and boiled and roasted. It was super-excellent.

¶

98th day

Weighed anchor and stood out to sea, bound to our last cruising station, the coast of Brazil. I leave this bleak, barren, uncultivated island with satisfaction. It affords no relief against the wearisomness of a long sea voyage.

It is now several weeks since all hands, including cabin-officers, were reduced to half-allowance. We find we have only sixty days' provision, even on this short allowance, and yet we expect to be at sea three months. I detest having my appetite limited. Nothing is more vexatious than to rise from table half-satisfied, with the pleasing anticipation of being soon reduced to a biscuit and half a pint of water per day. Who would not be a sailor?

¶

105th day

This morning saw a great number of Portuguese fishing boats, called iangarrs. These are perhaps the most singular water-vehicles ever invented by man. The natives of Brazil take five or six sharp-pointed logs, fasten them together, make a small bamboo mast, rig a light cotton latine sail, and thus navigate the great deep. The water makes a complete beach over them, or more properly they are under water continually, and secure themselves by railings from falling overboard. Yet with these aboriginal canoes they sail four or five knots per hour.

8 A.M. saw the land right ahead. The first appearance of the land is low, with a number of towers or churches along the coast.

10 A.M. Olinda and Pernambuco all in sight. The town of Olinda, six miles from Pernambuco, has a most beautiful

appearance as you approach it. The large white buildings scattered upon the sides of a lofty mountain and interspersed among the trees, with their steeples and cupolas, strike the eye with peculiar delight. Here the principal inhabitants have their country residences, and here most of the churches and convents are situated. The large city of Pernambuco occupies an extensive plain and with the numerous shipping in the harbour, adds greatly to this pleasurable sight. Besides you discover a great number of vessels approaching or leaving the coast, and two or three hundred of their iangarrs sailing up and down the coast, fishing, etc. At 11 A.M. jibed ship in pursuit of a sail to windward. How desponding it is to be in sight of such places as Olinda and Pernambuco, after being four months at sea, and not have it in our power to go on shore? Spoke a Portuguese schooner just out from Pernambuco, bound up the coast, who informed us, that there were no Englishmen of war on the coast, but three large English ships were taking in cargoes at Pernambuco.

It is worthy of remark that the *Yankee* sailed from Ascension to Cape St. Augustine, a distance of twelve hundred miles, in seven days and a half. During the whole time we had fresh trades, pleasant weather, a smooth sea, and all drawing sails set. We scarcely moved tack or sheet and never took in the studding sails during the whole run.

Ascension lies in Latitude 7° 55′ S.

Longitude 13.54′ W.

Cape St. Augustine in Latitude 8° 30′ S.

Longitude 35.40′ W.

¶

106th day
Capture of the Harriot & Matilda

Pernambuco being distant about 4 leagues.

At 1 P.M. piped all hands to quarters, cleared for action, run down under the lee of the large armed English brig, pierced for sixteen, and mounting eight eighteen-pound carronades, when within pistol shot, ordered the Enemy to strike his colours, he replied, "*I am all ready!*" Captain Wilson ordered his men not to fire and again commanded the enemy to lower his flag and quick the deck. He replied, "*Surely you are joking!*" Our commander still observing that the enemy was not prepared for action, prevented his men from firing and a third time ordered the enemy to strike, or he would sink him, which he now did with good reluctance. Sent our boat on board and found our prize to be the large armed letter of marque brig *Harriot & Matilda*, from Cork bound into Pernambuco, Captain John Inman, burthen 262 tons, coppered, with a full cargo of fine goods, crates, porter, cheese, butter, potatoes, etc. The *Harriott & Matilda* was formerly a Danish sloop of war, is a fine strong burthensome-vessel and sails well. This prize and cargo may be reasonably estimated at $45,000.

Here ends the second journal.